AGES 4-6

W9-ANZ-199

SCHOLASTIC

EARLY LEARNING

READY TO READ

Phonics • Sight Words • Word Families

New York • Toronto • London • Auckland • Sydney
Mexico City • New Delhi • Hong Kong • Buenos Aires

No part of this publication may be reproduced in whole or in part, or stored in a retrieval system, or transmitted in any form or by any means, electronic, mechanical, photocopying, recording, or otherwise, without written permission of the publisher. For information regarding permission, write to Scholastic Inc., 557 Broadway, New York, NY 10012.

Cover design: Tannaz Fassihi; Cover illustration: Jason Dove
Interior design: Michelle H. Kim
Interior illustration: Doug Jones

ISBN: 978-1-338-32317-7
Copyright © 2018 by Scholastic Inc.
All rights reserved.
Printed in the U.S.A.
First printing, September 2018.

3 4 5 6 7 8 9 10   56   24 23 22 21 20 19

Contents

Word Families

Sight Words

Dear Parent,

Thanks for choosing this workbook! For nearly a century, Scholastic has been a trusted leader in educational publishing. We firmly believe that it is never too early to begin the learning journey, especially when that journey includes delightful skill-building activities that are just right for young children.

On the pages that follow, you'll find hundreds of playful activities that are designed to keep your child engaged and challenged, but not overwhelmed. The book is organized into 30 sets, with each set focusing on a particular skill. (Turn the page for a list of skills.) Each set provides repeated practice to help your child gain confidence as he or she masters the skill.

Inside this book, you'll also find:

★ A handy chart at the beginning of each set to track your child's progress

★ 100+ colorful stickers (Helpful hint: Use these as rewards for completing each set.)

★ Ideas for fun family activities you can do with your child

★ A certificate of achievement to celebrate your child's accomplishments

The time is right to start your child on the path to a lifetime of reading success!

Sincerely,

The editors

Let's Get Ready to Read!

This activity book has been carefully designed to help ensure that your child has the tools he or she needs to excel in school. The formatted activities invite your child to read, trace, write, match, find, graph, and more! Your child will gain lots of experience with the target skill, helping to set the stage for reading success.

On the 200-plus pages that follow, you'll find plenty of practice with the following:

PHONICS

* short *a*
* short *e*
* short *i*
* short *o*
* short *u*

* long *a*
* long *e*
* long *i*
* long *o*
* long *u*

WORD FAMILIES

* –an, –at
* –ed, –ell
* –ick, –ing
* –ot, –ock
* –ug, –uck

* –am, –ap
* –ill, –ip
* –ail, –ake
* –ee, –eep
* –ice, –ight

SIGHT WORDS

* is, a, of, in
* and, the, to, you
* that, it, he, was
* she, for, are, as
* I, on, they, with

* be, at, have, this
* had, from, we, or
* said, words, not, what
* all, were, can, by
* but, one, when, your

Early Learning: Ready to Read is filled with motivating, special features including:

A handy chart at the start of each set that lets your child track his or her progress

Engaging activities that make learning fun

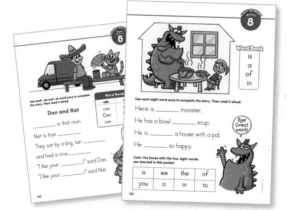

A review page that reinforces the target skill and can be used to assess your child's learning

Fun motivating stickers to celebrate your child's milestones

A certificate of achievement to reward your child's accomplishments

Tips for Using This Book

★ **Pick a good time** for your child to work. You may want to do it around mid-morning after play or early afternoon when your child is not too tired.

★ **Make sure your child has all the supplies** he or she needs, such as pencils and an eraser. Designate a special place for your child to work.

★ **Encourage your child to complete activities, but don't force the issue.** While you may want to ensure that your child succeeds, it's also important that he or she maintains a positive and relaxed attitude toward learning.

★ **Celebrate your child's accomplishments** by letting him or her affix stickers to completed sets of activities.

★ **Determine if your child needs help** completing the activity pages by giving him or her a few moments to review the page he or she will be working on. Then ask your child to describe what he or she will be doing on the pages. If your child needs support, try offering a choice about which family member might help. Giving your child a choice can help boost confidence and help him or her feel more ownership of the work to be done.

★ **Present your child with the certificate of achievement** on page 255 when he or she has completed the activity book. Feel free to frame or laminate the certificate and display it on the wall for everyone to see. Your child will be so proud!

EARLY LEARNING

PHONICS

fox

rock

pig

ring

Family Activities

Here are some skill-building activities that you and your child might enjoy.

Kitchen Words

On the refrigerator door, have a set of magnetic letters available for your child to use. While you prepare a meal, encourage your child to use the magnetic letters to spell words with long-vowel sounds and words with short-vowel sounds.

Word Search

Look for a long word, such as *caterpillar*, and challenge your child to find shorter words within the word. Challenge your child to tell you if the shorter word has a long- or short-vowel sound.

Words Can Add Up

As you read with your child, challenge him or her to find as many words as possible with short-vowel sounds. To make the game more fun, assign a point value to each vowel sound. For example, a short *a* can be worth one point and a short *e* can be worth five points. As your child identifies each short-vowel sound, add up the points. Repeat the challenge with long-vowel sounds. Keep a tally of points for the next time you play and encourage your child to better his or her score.

Two-Minute Lists

Give your child two minutes to list as many words as he or she can think of that contain a vowel sound of your choice. Then challenge your child to place the list in alphabetical order.

PHONICS
short a

Hi!

bat ~~bat~~

cap ~~cap~~

van ~~van~~

mad ~~mad~~

Trace each word above. Color in each box when you complete the activity.

1 Introduction	**2** Read & Write	**3** Read & Write	**4** Color
5 Graph	**6** Match & Find	**7** Unscramble	**8** Review

© Scholastic Inc.

Read the sentence.

The **bat** is **glad** he **has** a **cap**.

Trace and write the short-*a* words.

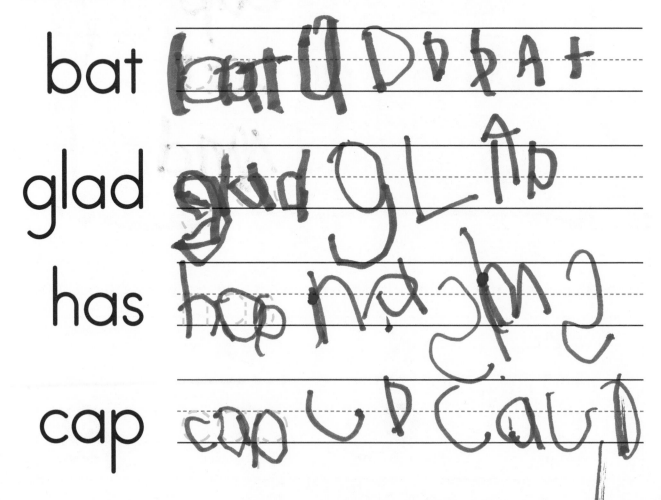

bat

glad

has

cap

© Scholastic Inc.

Read the sentence.

The bat is **mad** **at** **that** **cat**!

Trace and write the short-*a* words.

mad

at

that

cat

© Scholastic Inc.

Find the short-*a* words. Color them yellow .

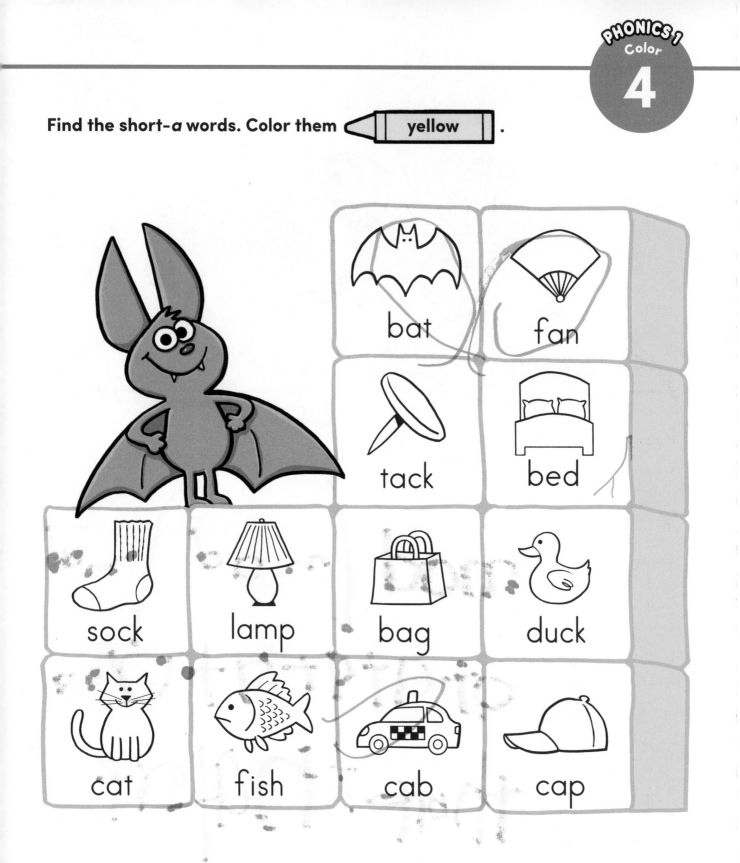

bat

fan

tack

bed

sock

lamp

bag

duck

cat

fish

cab

cap

How many blocks have short-*a* words? Circle the number.

1　2　3　4　5　6　7　8　9　10

© Scholastic Inc.

Count and graph the short-*a* words.

 bat	van	cab	mat

4

3

2

1

© Scholastic Inc.

Draw lines to match the bat with the short-*a* words.

ant •

fish •

cat •

lamp •

egg •

• pants

• doll

• fan

• bug

• pin

Find and circle each short-*a* word once.

Word Bank	
ant	e x l a m p b r
fan	a n t q v u x r
cat	v b o m f a n h
lamp	p l n c a t z c
pants	m r p a n t s d

© Scholastic Inc.

Unscramble each short-*a* word.

Word Bank	lamp	van	cat	bag
	mask	bat	man	ant

atb

nav

tac

sakm

pmal

abg

nam

nat

© Scholastic Inc.

Fill in each short-*a* word once to complete the story. Then read it aloud.

Word Bank   cat   sat   glad   ant   bat   cap

The New Cap

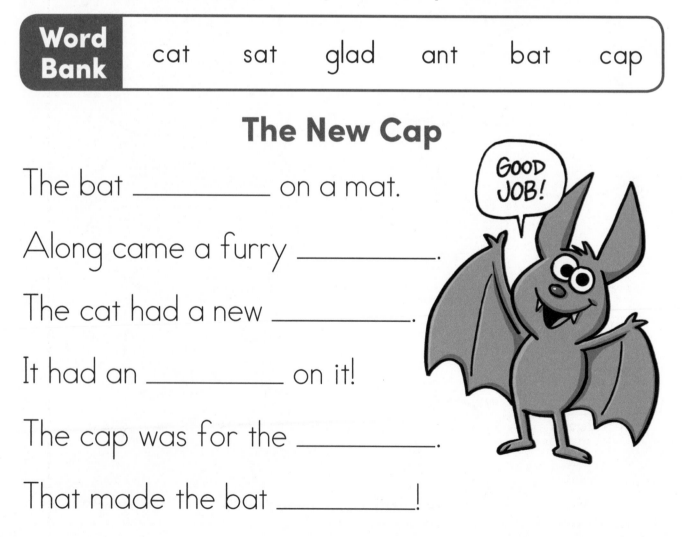

The bat _____ on a mat.

Along came a furry _____.

The cat had a new _____.

It had an _____ on it!

The cap was for the _____.

That made the bat _____!

18

© Scholastic Inc.

PHONICS
short e

Hi!

hen

bell

nest

elf

Trace each word above. Color in each box when you complete the activity.

1	**2**	**3**	**4**
Introduction	Read & Write	Read & Write	Color
5	**6**	**7**	**8**
Graph	Match & Find	Unscramble	Review

© Scholastic Inc.

Read the sentence.

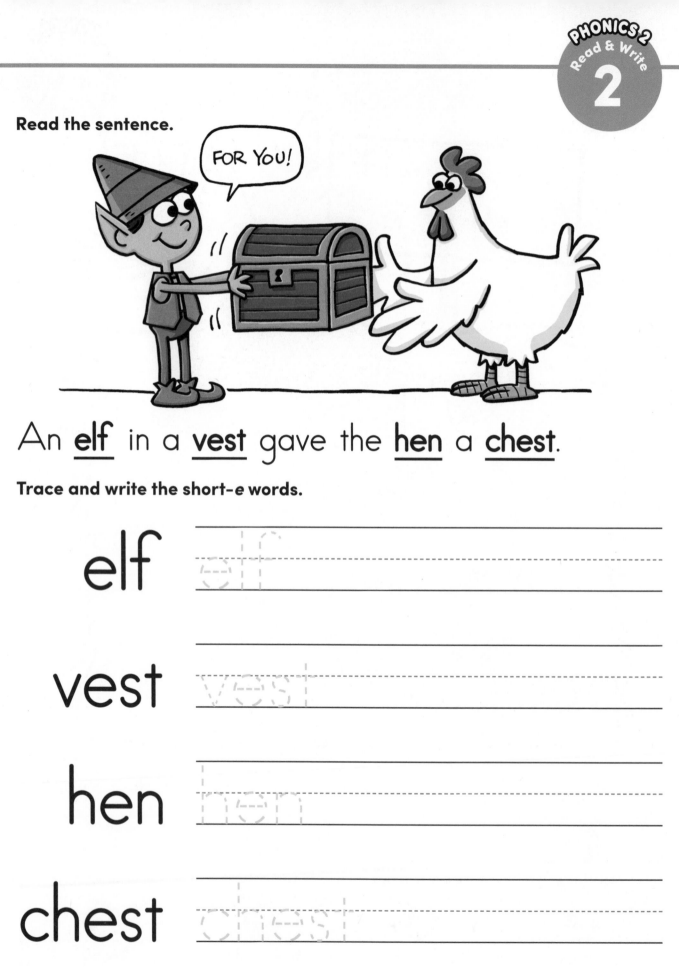

FOR YOU!

An <u>elf</u> in a <u>vest</u> gave the <u>hen</u> a <u>chest</u>.

Trace and write the short-*e* words.

elf

vest

hen

chest

© Scholastic Inc.

Read the sentence.

A <u>**shell**</u>, <u>**pen**</u>, <u>**bell**</u>, and <u>**dress**</u> were in the chest.

Trace and write the short-*e* words.

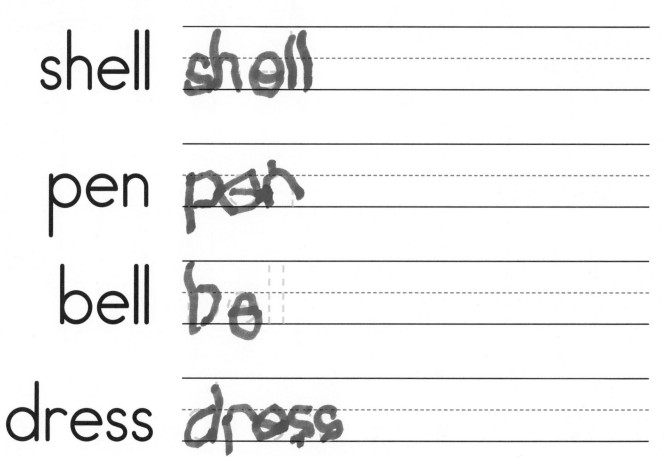

shell

pen

bell

dress

© Scholastic Inc.

Find the short-*e* words. Color them blue .

hen

egg

nest

cat

dog

vest

shell

tent

mug

bag

ten

pig

How many blocks have short-*e* words? Circle the number.

1   2   3   4   5   6   7   8   9   10

© Scholastic Inc.

Count and graph the short-*e* words.

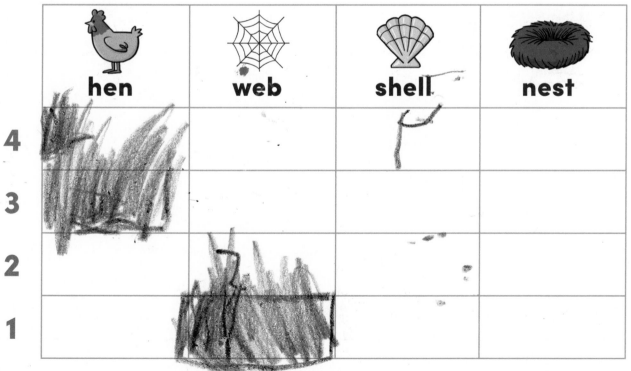

hen	web	shell	nest

© Scholastic Inc.

Draw lines to match the hen with the short-*e* words.

clock •

bed •

egg •

bug •

tent •

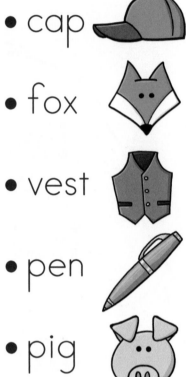

• cap

• fox

• vest

• pen

• pig

Find and circle each short-*e* word once.

Word Bank	
vest	y c t e n t a d
bed	b e d t z u m n
egg	q k o p f p e n
pen	r a s e g g n h
tent	u g c v e s t i

© Scholastic Inc.

Unscramble each short-*e* word.

| **Word Bank** | hen | elf | egg | leg |
| | tent | web | vest | nest |

svet

_____

geg

_____

snet

_____

fle

_____

bew

_____

nett

_____

neh

_____

gle

_____

© Scholastic Inc.

Fill in each short-*e* word once to complete the story. Then read it aloud.

Word Bank | hen   elf   pen   then   dress   end

The Best Chest

The red _____ got the best chest!

It was from the _____.

A dress and _____ were in it.

The hen wore the _____

and _____ she wrote a note

with the pen. The _____.

© Scholastic Inc.

PHONICS short *i*

Hi!

pig

bib

fish

ring

Trace each word above. Color in each box when you complete the activity.

1 Introduction	2 Read & Write	3 Read & Write	4 Color
5 Graph	6 Match & Find	7 Unscramble	8 Review

© Scholastic Inc.

Read the sentence.

The **pig** **is** in a very **big** **wig**.

Trace and write the short-*i* words.

pig

is

big

wig

© Scholastic Inc.

Read the sentence.

The pig **in** the wig wears a **bib** to **lick** **six** lollipops.

Trace and write the short-*i* words.

in

bib

lick

six

© Scholastic Inc.

Find the short-*i* words. Color them ▸ pink .

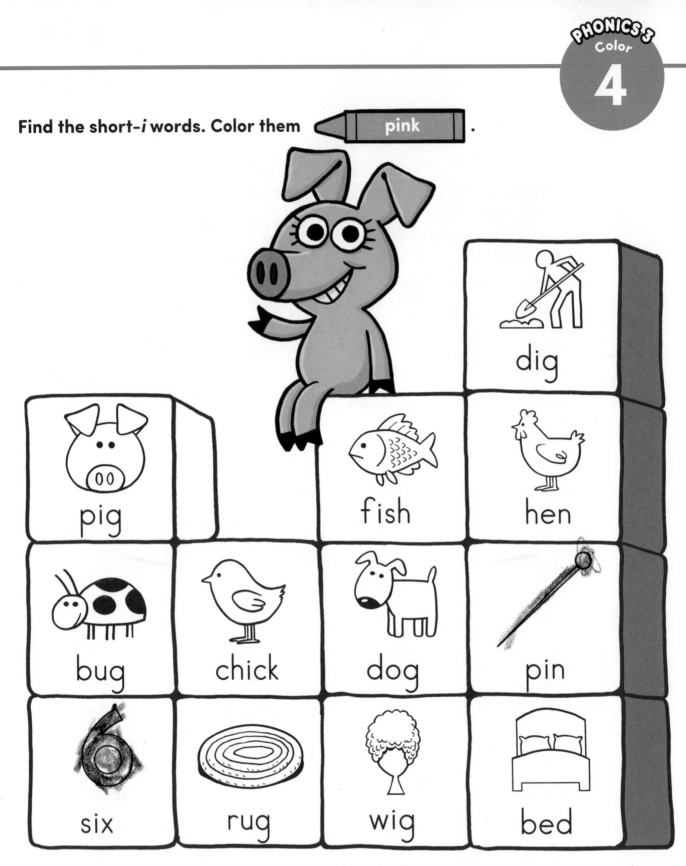

dig

pig

fish

hen

bug

chick

dog

pin

six

rug

wig

bed

How many blocks have short-*i* words? Circle the number.

1   2   3   4   5   6   7   8   9   10

© Scholastic Inc.

Count and graph the short-*i* words.

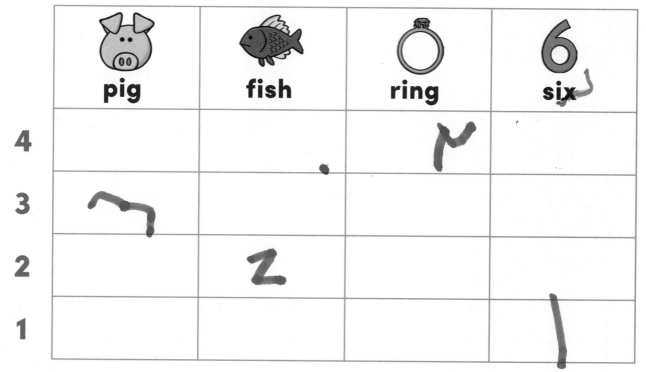

	pig	fish	ring	six
4			ﻥ	
3	⌐			
2		Z		
1				ﺍ

© Scholastic Inc.

Draw lines to match the pig with the short-*i* words.

ring •

rug •

dig •

mop •

fish •

• bat

• pin

• kid

• clock

• bag

Find and circle each short-*i* word once.

Word Bank	e c f i s h k d
ring	t d i g t y o b
kid	d y u x p i n j
dig	k i d n q e d v
fish	b a r i n g m z
pin	

© Scholastic Inc.

Unscramble each short-*i* word.

Word Bank

pig	kid	wig	pin
ring	six	fish	bib

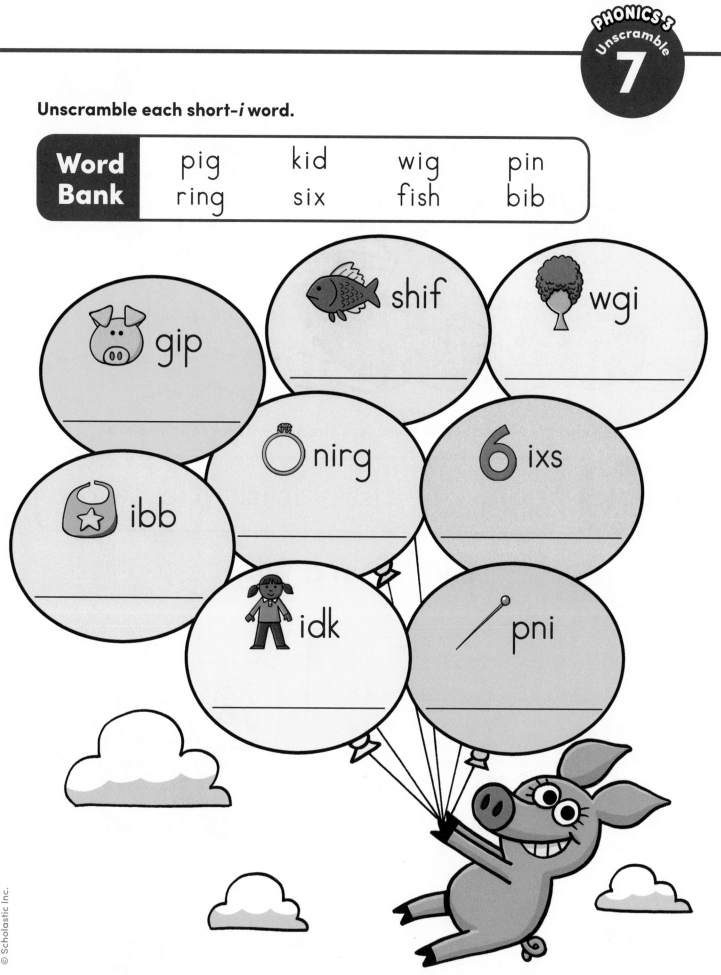

gip

shif

wgi

ibb

nirg

6 ixs

idk

pni

© Scholastic Inc.

Fill in each short-*i* word once to complete the story. Then read it aloud.

Word Bank   pig   in   fish   Splish   kid   wig

The Pig in a Wig

"Oink!" said the _____.

She was _____ a boat

with a nice _____.

_____, splash!

A _____ jumped up!

The fish has a big _____, too!

34

© Scholastic Inc.

PHONICS
short o

dog

fox

rock

mop

Trace each word above. Color in each box when you complete the activity.

1 Introduction	2 Read & Write	3 Read & Write	4 Color
5 Graph	6 Match & Find	7 Unscramble	8 Review

© Scholastic Inc.

Read the sentence.

The <u>dog</u> and <u>frog</u> sit <u>on</u> a <u>log</u>.

Trace and write the short-*o* words.

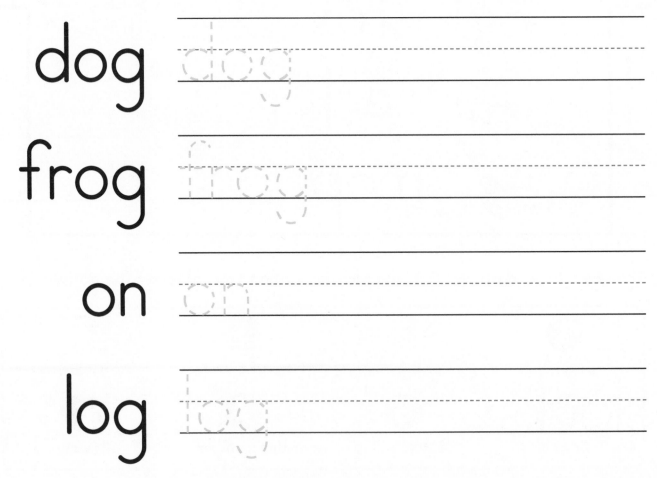

dog

frog

on

log

© Scholastic Inc.

Read the sentence.

A <u>fox</u> gave them a <u>box</u> with <u>lots</u> of <u>clocks</u>.

Trace and write the short-*o* words.

fox

box

lots

clocks

© Scholastic Inc.

Find the short-*o* words. Color them green .

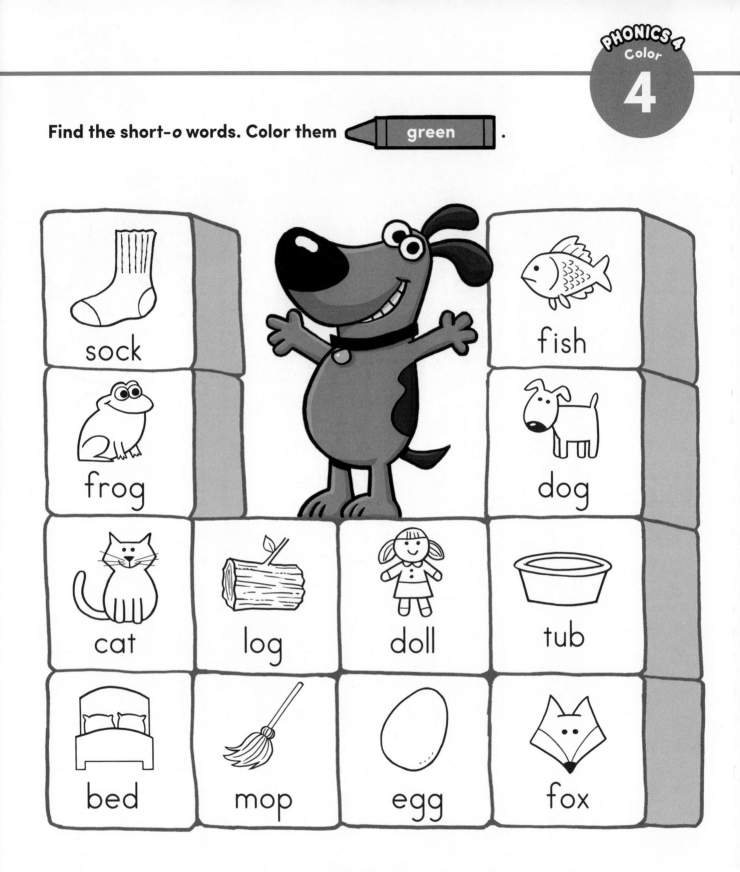

sock

frog

fish

dog

cat

log

doll

tub

bed

mop

egg

fox

How many blocks have short-*o* words? Circle the number.

1 2 3 4 5 6 7 8 9 10

© Scholastic Inc.

Count and graph the short-*o* words.

dog   fox   dog

                rock

    fox   dog

        rock   dog

  fox   stop

	🐕 dog	🦊 fox	🪨 rock	🛑 stop
4				
3				
2				
1				

© Scholastic Inc.

Draw lines to match the dog with the short-*o* words.

bell •

clock •

pig •

bag •

mop •

• log

• cup

• duck

• frog

• box

Find and circle each short-*o* word once.

Word Bank	
frog	c g a b o x k d
mop	q t c l o c k n
clock	w e r x m o p u
log	l o g m s e t v
box	u r f r o g z f

© Scholastic Inc.

Unscramble each short-*o* word.

Word Bank	fox	frog	ox	doll
	mop	rock	pot	sock

kcos

fxo
_____

cokr
_____

xo
_____

pmo
_____

llod
_____

opt
_____

grof
_____

© Scholastic Inc.

41

Fill in each short-*o* word once to complete the story. Then read it aloud.

Word Bank	lots	tock	doll	dog	sock	of

The Box of Clocks

Fox gave _____ and frog a box.

The box had _____ of clocks!

Some _____ the clocks were silly.

One clock looked like a pretty _____!

One clock looked like a stinky _____!

Tick, _____!

42

© Scholastic Inc.

PHONICS
short *u*

Hi!

duck

bus

gum

sun

Trace each word above. Color in each box when you complete the activity.

1 Introduction	2 Read & Write	3 Read & Write	4 Color
5 Graph	6 Match & Find	7 Unscramble	8 Review

© Scholastic Inc.

Read the sentence.

A **duck** in a **truck** saw his pals **run** to get the **bus**.

Trace and write the short-*u* words.

duck

truck

run

bus

© Scholastic Inc.

Read the sentence.

The duck told the **pup** and **skunk** to **just** **jump** in his truck.

Trace and write the short-*u* words.

pup

skunk

just

jump

© Scholastic Inc.

Find the short-*u* words. Color them orange **.**

duck

bug

jug

bag

rock

bus

web

mug

rug

pig

skunk

pup

How many blocks have short-*u* words? Circle the number.

1   2   3   4   5   6   7   8   9   10

© Scholastic Inc.

Count and graph the short-*u* words.

duck	**sun**	**bus**	**gum**

4				
3				
2				
1				

© Scholastic Inc.

Draw lines to match the duck with the short-*u* words.

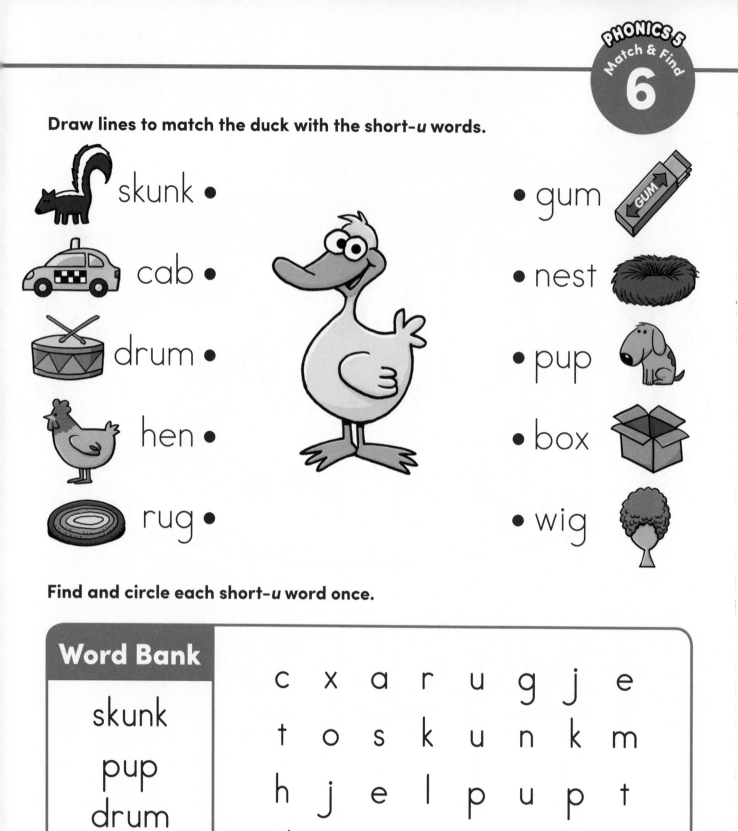

skunk •

cab •

drum •

hen •

rug •

• gum

• nest

• pup

• box

• wig

Find and circle each short-*u* word once.

Word Bank	
skunk	c x a r u g j e
pup	t o s k u n k m
drum	h j e l p u p t
gum	d r u m z i n v
rug	c a d g u m t i

© Scholastic Inc.

Unscramble each short-*u* word.

Word Bank

duck	jug	bug	pup
drum	bus	cup	truck

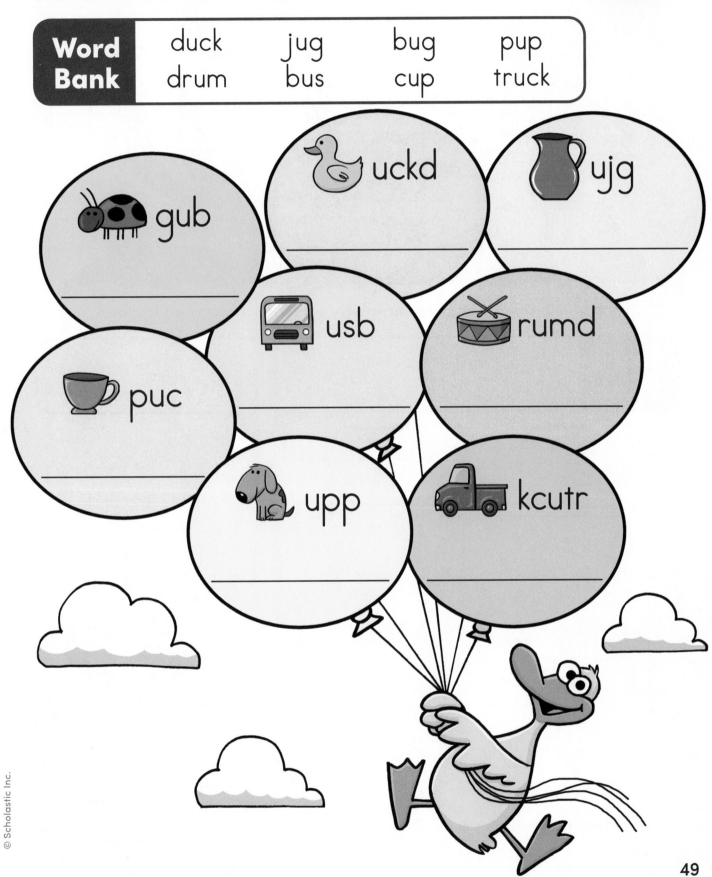

gub _____

uckd _____

ujg _____

puc _____

usb _____

rumd _____

upp _____

kcutr _____

© Scholastic Inc.

Fill in each short-*u* word once to complete the story. Then read it aloud.

Word Bank	up	fun	duck	cups	yum	sun

Up the Hill

The _____, pup, and skunk

went _____ a big hill.

Then they sat in the warm _____

and drank _____ of tea.

Yum, _____!

It was so _____!

GOOD JOB!

© Scholastic Inc.

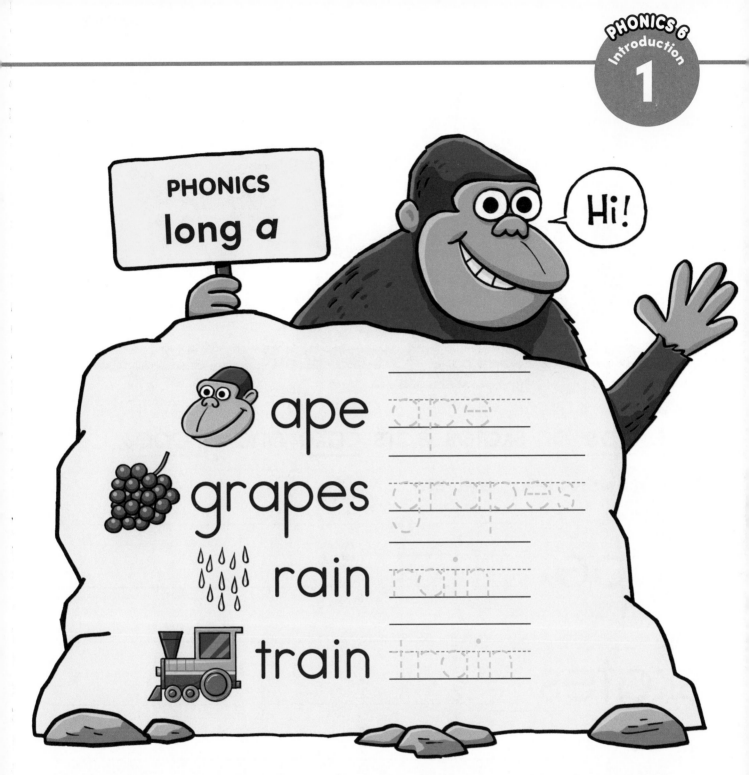

PHONICS
long a

Hi!

ape

grapes

rain

train

Trace each word above. Color in each box when you complete the activity.

1 Introduction	2 Read & Write	3 Read & Write	4 Color
5 Graph	6 Match & Find	7 Unscramble	8 Review

© Scholastic Inc.

Read the sentence.

The **ape** on **skates** eats **cake** and **grapes**.

Trace and write the long-*a* words.

ape

skates

cake

grapes

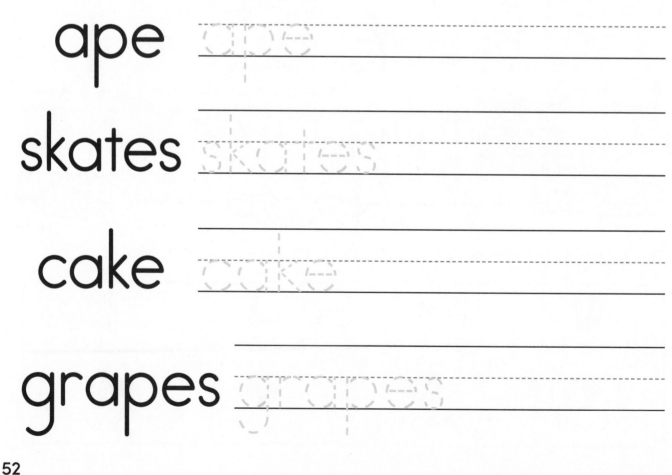

© Scholastic Inc.

Read the sentence.

The ape plays with his **train**, **snail**, and **pail** in the **rain**.

Trace and write the long-*a* words.

train

snail

pail

rain

© Scholastic Inc.

Find the long-*a* words. Color them red .

ape

pail

rain

cave

cake

tail

bee

fox

truck

ring

grapes

pig

How many blocks have long-*a* words? Circle the number.

1   2   3   4   5   6   7   8   9   10

© Scholastic Inc.

Count and graph the long-*a* words.

 ape	plane	train	paint
4			
3			
2			
1			

© Scholastic Inc.

Draw lines to match the ape with the long-*a* words.

kite •

cake •

mule •

feet •

train •

• bike

• wave

• gate

• rope

• snake

Find and circle each long-*a* word once.

Word Bank	
snake	t r a i n p b r
cake	a n t q c a k e
gate	v g a t e a n d
wave	p l s n a k e c
train	m r p w a v e x

© Scholastic Inc.

Unscramble each long-*a* word.

Word Bank	pail	snake	wave	cake
	rain	snail	ape	nail

pae _____

ekac _____

vwae _____

anir _____

lasin _____

naske _____

liap _____

ilan _____

© Scholastic Inc.

Fill in each long-*a* word once to complete the story. Then read it aloud.

Word Bank ape whale gave paint made snail

Ape's Painting

The _____ is an artist.

He loves to _____.

He _____ a picture

of a _____ in the rain.

He _____ it to the snail.

"I love it!" said the _____.

© Scholastic Inc.

**PHONICS
long e**

Hi!

seal

leaf

bee

tree

Trace each word above. Color in each box when you complete the activity.

| **1** Introduction | **2** Read & Write | **3** Read & Write | **4** Color |
| **5** Graph | **6** Match & Find | **7** Unscramble | **8** Review |

© Scholastic Inc.

Read the sentence.

The **seal** likes to **eat** ice **cream** on the **beach**.

Trace and write the long-*e* words.

seal

eat

cream

beach

© Scholastic Inc.

Read the sentence.

The seal goes to **sleep** and dreams about **three** **bees** and **cheese**.

Trace and write the long-*e* words.

sleep

three

bees

cheese

© Scholastic Inc.

Find the long-*e* words. Color them `purple` .

seal

tree

beach

mice

queen

skate

feet

leaf

bee

boat

jeans

cube

How many blocks have long-e words? Circle the number.

1   2   3   4   5   6   7   8   9   10

© Scholastic Inc.

Count and graph the long-*e* words.

seal
jeep
teeth
cheese
teeth
jeep
jeep
teeth
seal
teeth

	seal	jeep	cheese	teeth
4				
3				
2				
1				

© Scholastic Inc.

Draw lines to match the seal with the long-*e* words.

queen •

grapes •

feet •

bike •

cube •

• peach

• jeans

• skate

• phone

• tree

Find and circle each long-*e* word once.

Word Bank								
queen	i	y	p	e	a	c	h	o
jeans	x	t	r	e	e	s	u	k
peach	v	h	f	e	e	t	n	d
feet	w	o	g	j	e	a	n	s
tree	q	u	e	e	n	p	x	z

© Scholastic Inc.

Unscramble each long-*e* word.

Word Bank	bee	jeep	leaf	feet
	cheese	seal	wheel	sheep

lase

_____

efet

_____

fael

_____

eeechs

_____

ebe

_____

eehwl

_____

epje

_____

heeps

_____

© Scholastic Inc.

Fill in each long-e word once to complete the story. Then read it aloud.

Word Bank	beach	queen	jeep
	sea	beep	sheep

Seal at the Beach

Seal is at a sandy _____.

He sees a _____

standing in the _____.

He sees a queen driving

in a _____.

The _____ toots her horn.

Beep, _____!

GOOD JOB!

© Scholastic Inc.

Trace each word above. Color in each box when you complete the activity.

1 Introduction	2 Read & Write	3 Read & Write	4 Color
5 Graph	6 Match & Find	7 Unscramble	8 Review

© Scholastic Inc.

Read the sentence.

The **<u>mice</u> <u>ride</u>** a **<u>bike</u>** as the sun **<u>shines</u>**.

Trace and write the long-*i* words.

mice

ride

bike

shines

© Scholastic Inc.

Read the sentence.

The **nice** mice fly **five kites** near a **slide**.

Trace and write the long-*i* words.

nice

five

kites

slide

© Scholastic Inc.

Find the long-*i* words. Color them ▬▬ brown ▬▬ .

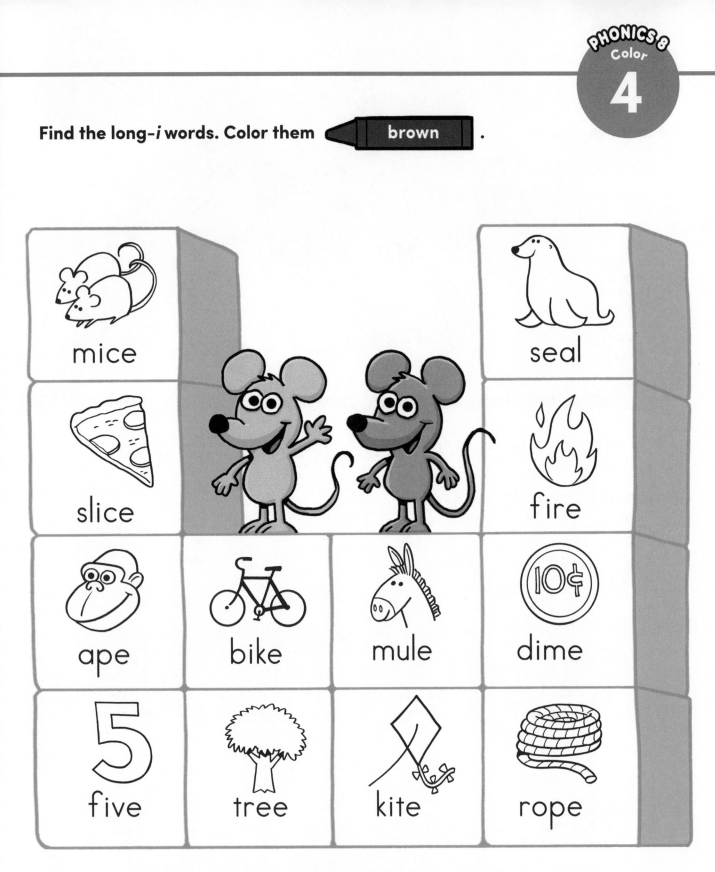

mice

slice

seal

fire

ape

bike

mule

dime

five

tree

kite

rope

How many blocks have long-*i* words? Circle the number.

1 2 3 4 5 6 7 8 9 10

© Scholastic Inc.

Count and graph the long-*i* words.

 mice	kite	9 nine	10¢ dime
4			
3			
2			
1			

© Scholastic Inc.

Draw lines to match the mice with the long-*i* words.

queen •

hive •

jeep •

nine •

mule •

• bike

• kite

• plate

• coat

• five **5**

Find and circle each long-*i* word once.

Word Bank	
bike	h i v e m p b r
hive	a n i n e u x r
nine	v b o m k i t e
kite	p b i k e t z c
five	m r f i v e s d

© Scholastic Inc.

Unscramble each long-*i* word.

Word Bank	mice	rice	tire	kite
	ice	fire	nine	hive

cime _____

evih _____

cie _____

teki _____

riet _____

erif _____

9 nnei _____

ceir _____

© Scholastic Inc.

Fill in each long-*i* word once to complete the story. Then read it aloud.

Word Bank   like   dive   slide   cried   mice   nice

The Nice Pool Party

GOOD JOB!

"What a _____ day for

a pool party!" said the _____.

One mouse did a fine _____.

One mouse slid down a _____.

"We really _____ playing

in the water!" they _____.

© Scholastic Inc.

PHONICS
long o

Hi!

goat

boat

nose

rope

Trace each word above. Color in each box when you complete the activity.

1	2	3	4
Introduction	**Read & Write**	**Read & Write**	**Color**
5	6	7	8
Graph	**Match & Find**	**Unscramble**	**Review**

© Scholastic Inc.

Read the sentence.

The **goat** wears a **coat** when he **floats** in a **boat**.

Trace and write the long-*o* words.

goat

coat

floats

boat

© Scholastic Inc.

Read the sentence.

The goat sees an **old toad** with a **rose** in a **slow** boat.

Trace and write the long-*o* words.

old

toad

rose

slow

© Scholastic Inc.

Find the long-*o* words. Color them grey **.**

goat

coat

boat

globe

road

queen

cake

toast

cone

plate

rose

kite

How many blocks have long-*o* words? Circle the number.

1 2 3 4 5 6 7 8 9 10

© Scholastic Inc.

Count and graph the long-*o* words.

 goat	 soap	 rose	 smoke

(rows labeled)
4
3
2
1

© Scholastic Inc.

Draw lines to match the goat with the long-*o* words.

soap •

bike •

phone •

jeep •

rope •

• cube

• boat

• nose

• rain

• snail

Find and circle each long-*o* word once.

Word Bank	
boat	r o p e k e q z
soap	a b h s o a p w
phone	g p h o n e i d
nose	n o s e m y u t
rope	t g a b o a t c

© Scholastic Inc.

Unscramble each long-o word.

Word Bank	nose soap rope road
	boat goat phone hole

taog

posa
_____

atob
_____

_____

poer
_____

adro
_____

seno

leho
_____

enoph
_____

_____

© Scholastic Inc.

Fill in each long-*o* word once to complete the story. Then read it aloud.

Word Bank | phone   goat   joke   toad   so   boat

The Goat in a Boat

The goat in a _____

uses his cell _____

to call the old _____.

Then the _____

tells the old toad a _____.

The joke is _____ funny!

© Scholastic Inc.

PHONICS
long _u_

Hi!

mule
cube
flute
human

Trace each word above. Color in each box when you complete the activity.

1 Introduction	2 Read & Write	3 Read & Write	4 Color
5 Graph	6 Match & Find	7 Unscramble	8 Review

© Scholastic Inc.

Read the sentence.

The <u>cute mule</u> stood on a <u>huge cube</u>.

Trace and write the long-*u* words.

cute

mule

huge

cube

© Scholastic Inc.

Read the sentence.

The mule **used** a **flute** to play **music** for a **unicorn**.

Trace and write the long-*u* words.

used

flute

music

unicorn

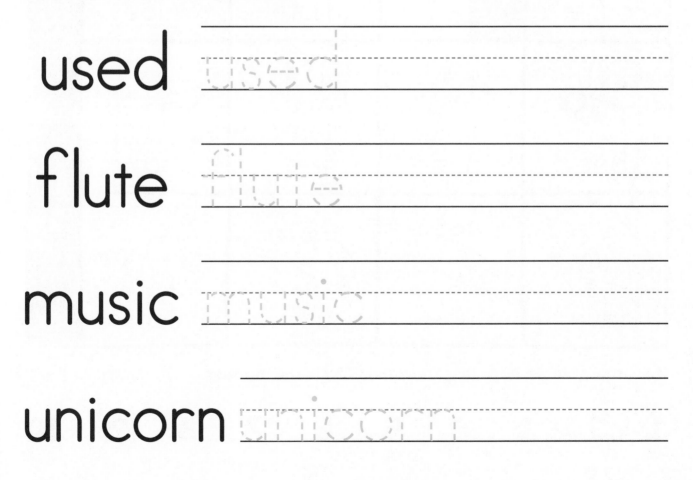

© Scholastic Inc.

Find the long-*u* words. Color them blue .

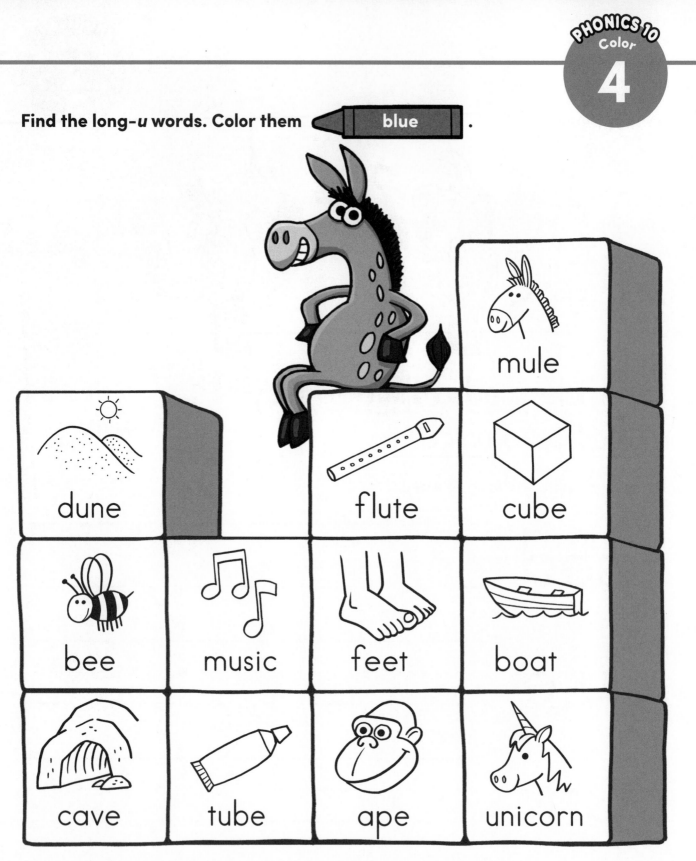

mule

dune

flute

cube

bee

music

feet

boat

cave

tube

ape

unicorn

How many blocks have long-*u* words? Circle the number.

1   2   3   4   5   6   7   8   9   10

© Scholastic Inc.

Count and graph the long-*u* words.

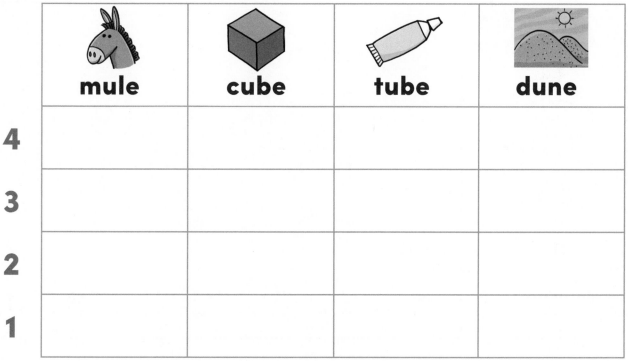

	![mule]	![cube]	![tube]	![dune]
	mule	**cube**	**tube**	**dune**
4				
3				
2				
1				

© Scholastic Inc.

Draw lines to match the mule with the long-*u* words.

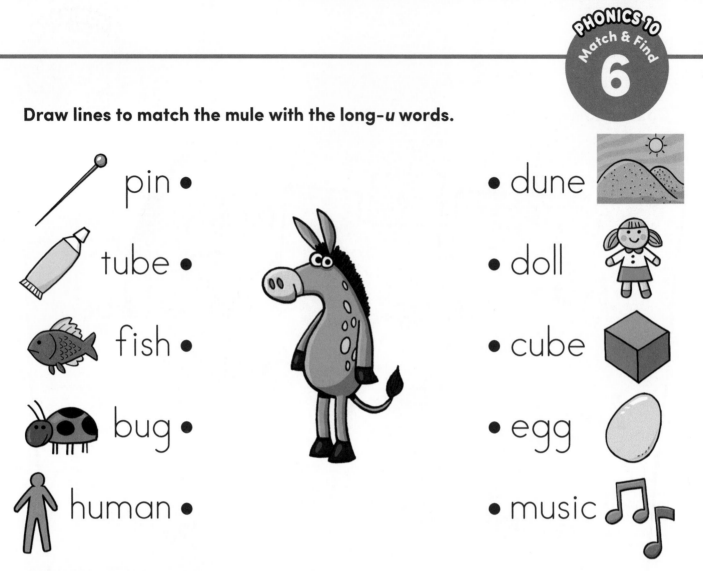

pin •

tube •

fish •

bug •

human •

• dune

• doll

• cube

• egg

• music

Find and circle each long-*u* word once.

Word Bank	
cube tube dune music human	d u n e s i m x d h c u b e q r k h u m a n o t t u b e n y a r h y m u s i c d

© Scholastic Inc.

Unscramble each long-*u* word.

Word Bank

mule	bugle	dune	cube
flute	music	tube	unicorn

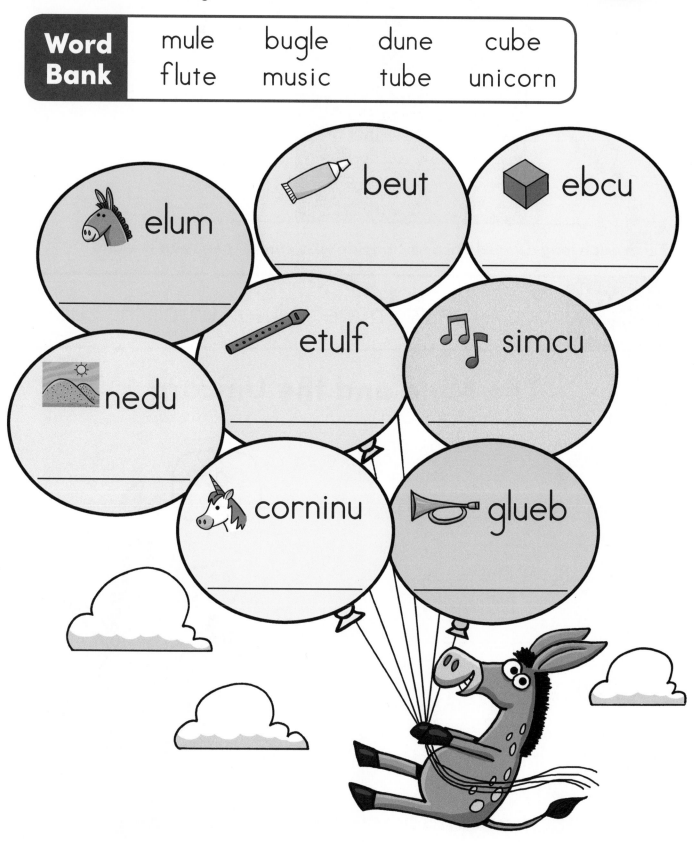

elum

beut

ebcu

nedu

etulf

simcu

corninu

glueb

© Scholastic Inc.

Fill in each long-*u* word once to complete the story. Then read it aloud.

Word Bank	bugle mule huge flute unicorn cube

The Mule and the Unicorn

The _____ has spots!

The _____ has stars!

They sit on a _____.

It is so _____!

The mule plays a _____.

The unicorn plays a _____.

They make beautiful music!

GOOD JOB!

© Scholastic Inc.

Family Activities

Here are some skill-building activities that you and your child might enjoy.

Making Words

On a small chalkboard or whiteboard, write new words with the same word family. For example, starting with the word *cat*, erase the *c* and encourage your child to write a different consonant in its place to make a new word, such as *hat, bat,* or *mat*. Make sure all the words used are real.

Two-Minute Lists

Give your child two minutes to list as many words in a given word family as he or she can think of.

Let's Jump Rope!

As your child jumps rope, call out a phonogram and encourage him or her to say as many words as he or she can think of in that word family. For example, if you call out *–ing* your child might respond with *king, ring, wing.*

Silly Sentences

On sticky notes, write words within the same word family. For example, write *then, when, den, men, ten*. Challenge your child to create silly sentences using the words on the sticky notes. Give your child 3 to 4 blank sticky notes for additional words.

Fill in the -an and -at words.

Hi!

WORD FAMILIES
-an, -at

DAN

NAT

-an	-at
m_____	c_____
v_____	b_____
f_____	m_____

Color in each box when you complete an activity.

1 Introduction -an & -at	**2** Read & Write -an	**3** Match & Find -an	**4** Graph -an
5 Read & Write -at	**6** Match & Find -at	**7** Graph -at	**8** Review -an & -at

© Scholastic Inc.

Read the sentence.
Then write the words.

A <u>man</u> named <u>Dan</u> drives a big <u>van</u>.

man

Dan

van

Use the letters to make more -an words.

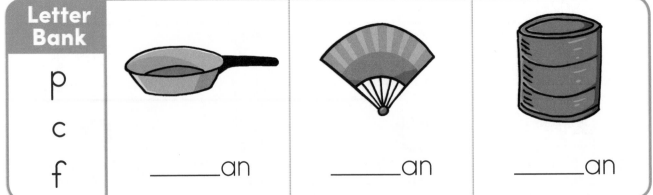

Letter Bank			
p			
c	____an	____an	____an
f			

© Scholastic Inc.

Match the -an words to their pictures.

man •

pan •

van •

can •

fan •

•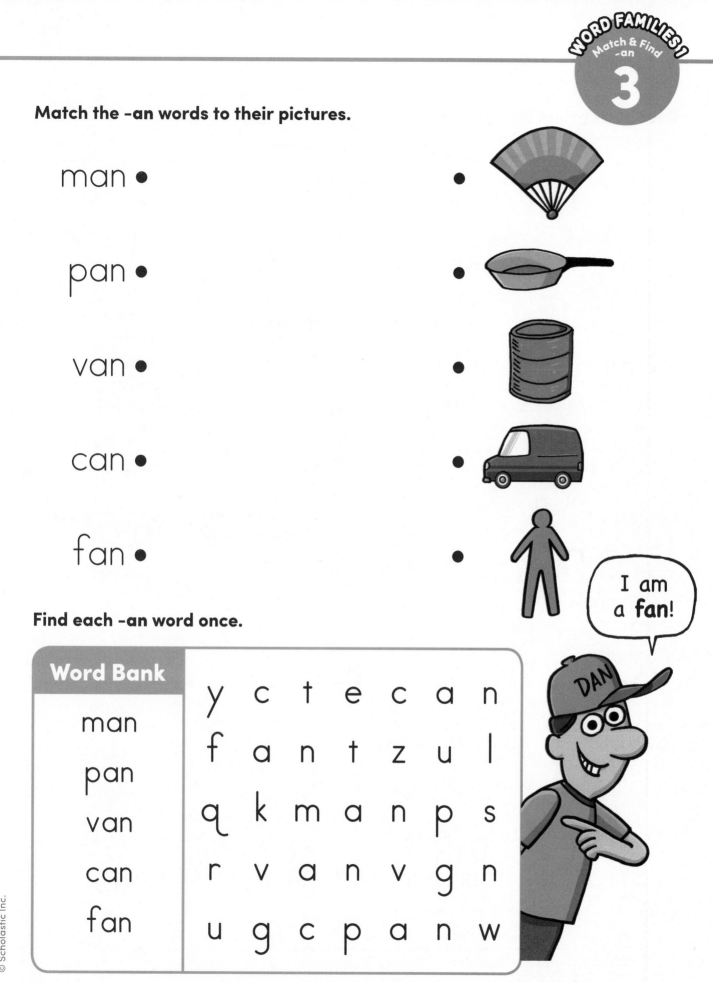

•

•

•

•

I am a **fan**!

Find each -an word once.

Word Bank	
man	y c t e c a n
pan	f a n t z u l
van	q k m a n p s
can	r v a n v g n
fan	u g c p a n w

DAN

© Scholastic Inc.

Count and graph the -an words.

Math is fun!

tan   man

fan   tan

pan   tan   pan

tan   fan   pan

	 man	 fan	TAN tan	 pan
4				
3				
2				
1				

I found this –an word the most times:

_____

© Scholastic Inc.

WORD FAMILIES 1
Read & Write
-at
5

**Read the sentence.
Then write the words.**

The **cat** **sat** with a nice **bat**.

cat cat

sat sat

bat bat

Use the letters to make more -at words.

Letter Bank

p

r

h

____at   ____at   ____at

© Scholastic Inc.

Match the -at words to their pictures.

cat •

rat •

hat •

mat •

bat •

Find each -at word once.

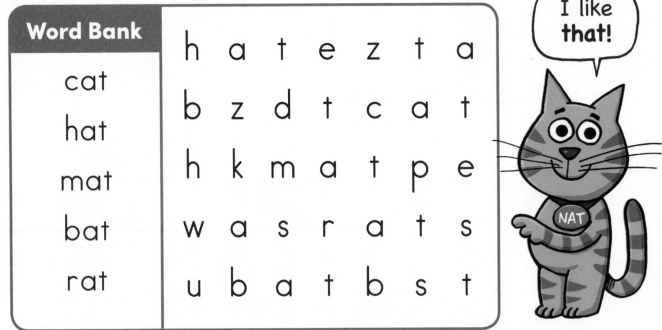

Word Bank							
cat	h	a	t	e	z	t	a
hat	b	z	d	t	c	a	t
mat	h	k	m	a	t	p	e
bat	w	a	s	r	a	t	s
rat	u	b	a	t	b	s	t

I like that!

NAT

© Scholastic Inc.

Count and graph the -at words.

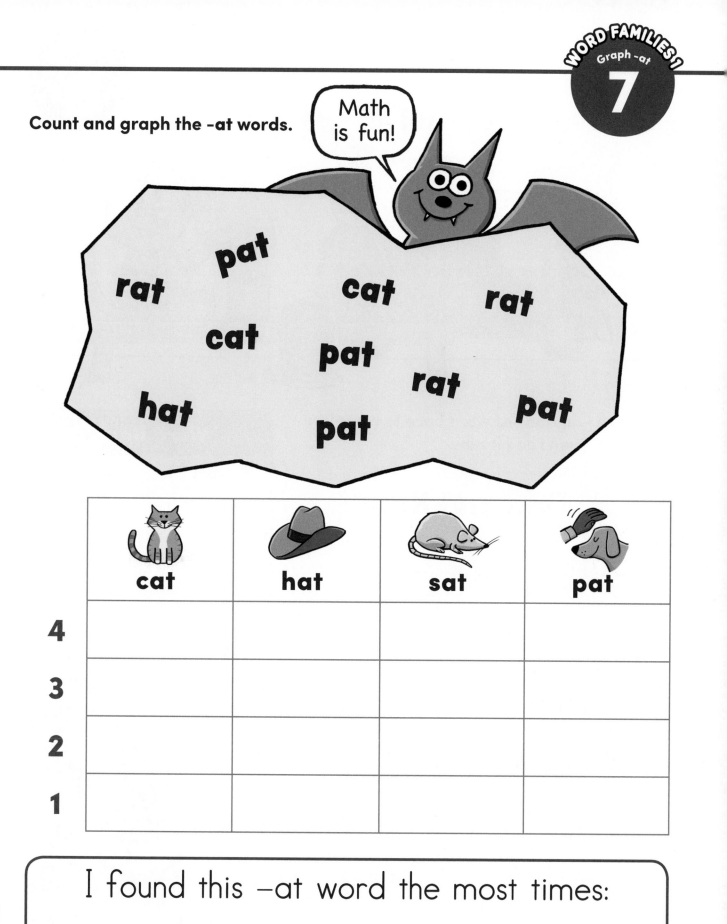

Math is fun!

	cat	hat	sat	pat
4				
3				
2				
1				

I found this –at word the most times:

_____

© Scholastic Inc.

Use each -an and -at word once to complete the story. Then read it aloud.

Dan and Nat

_____ is that man.

Nat is that _____.

They sat by a big, tan _____

and had a nice_____.

"I like your _____!" said Dan.

"I like your _____!" said Nat.

Word Bank

-an	-at
can	cat
Dan	that
van	fan

Great work! Bye!

© Scholastic Inc.

Fill in the -ed and -ell words.

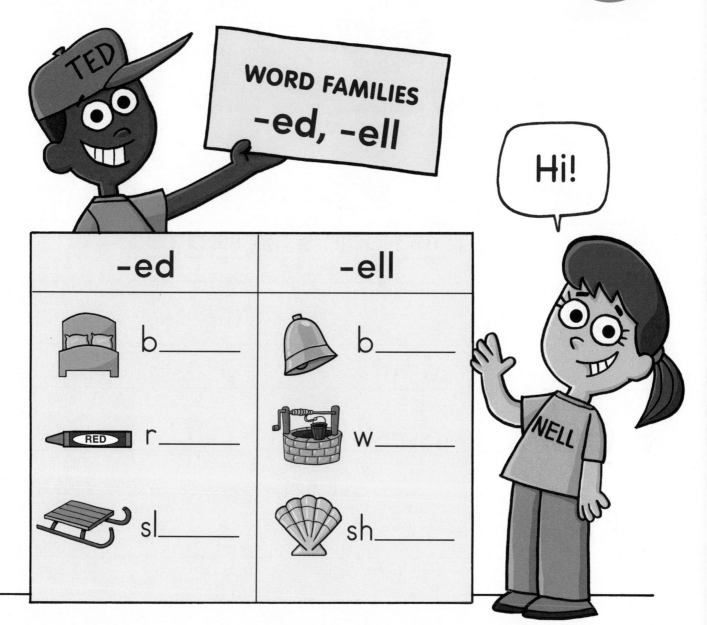

WORD FAMILIES
-ed, -ell

Hi!

-ed	-ell
b_____	b_____
r_____	w_____
sl_____	sh_____

Color in each box when you complete an activity.

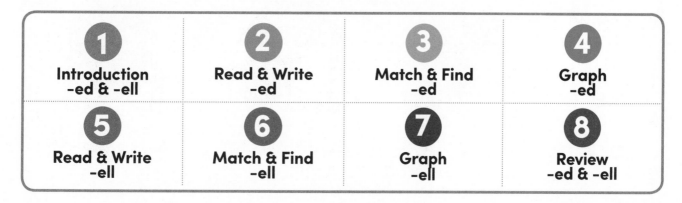

1 Introduction -ed & -ell	2 Read & Write -ed	3 Match & Find -ed	4 Graph -ed
5 Read & Write -ell	6 Match & Find -ell	7 Graph -ell	8 Review -ed & -ell

© Scholastic Inc.

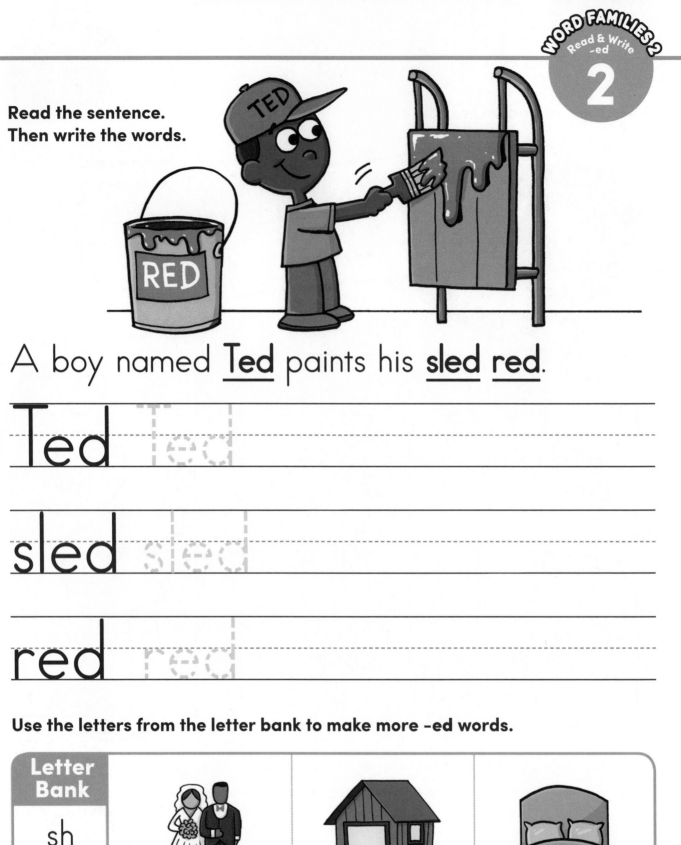

**Read the sentence.
Then write the words.**

A boy named **Ted** paints his **sled red**.

Ted

sled

red

Use the letters from the letter bank to make more -ed words.

Letter Bank			
sh			
w	____ed	____ed	____ed
b			

© Scholastic Inc.

Match the -ed words to their pictures.

red •

bed •

sled •

wed •

shed •

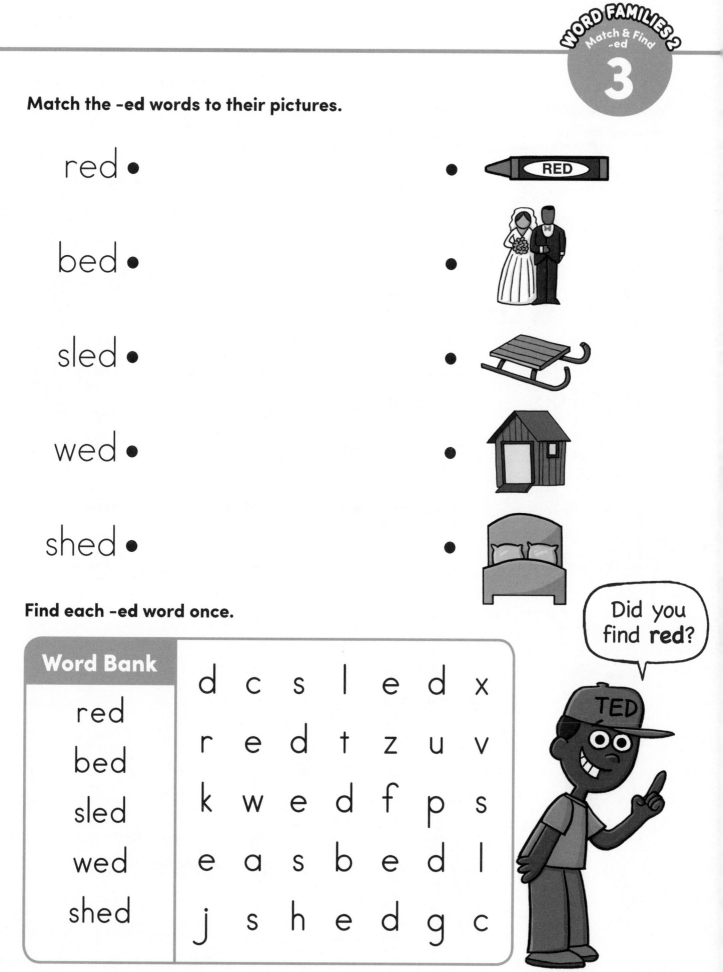

• RED

•

•

•

•

Find each -ed word once.

Word Bank	
red	d c s l e d x
bed	r e d t z u v
sled	k w e d f p s
wed	e a s b e d l
shed	j s h e d g c

Did you find **red**?

TED

© Scholastic Inc.

Count and graph the -ed words.

Math is fun!

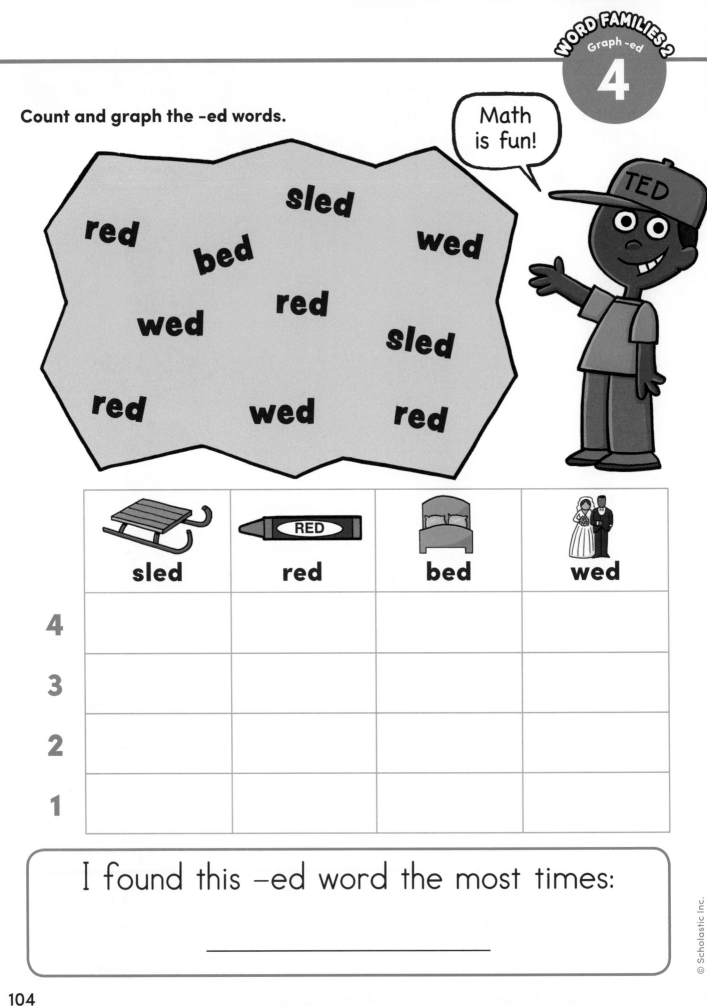

red

sled

bed

wed

wed

red

sled

red

wed

red

	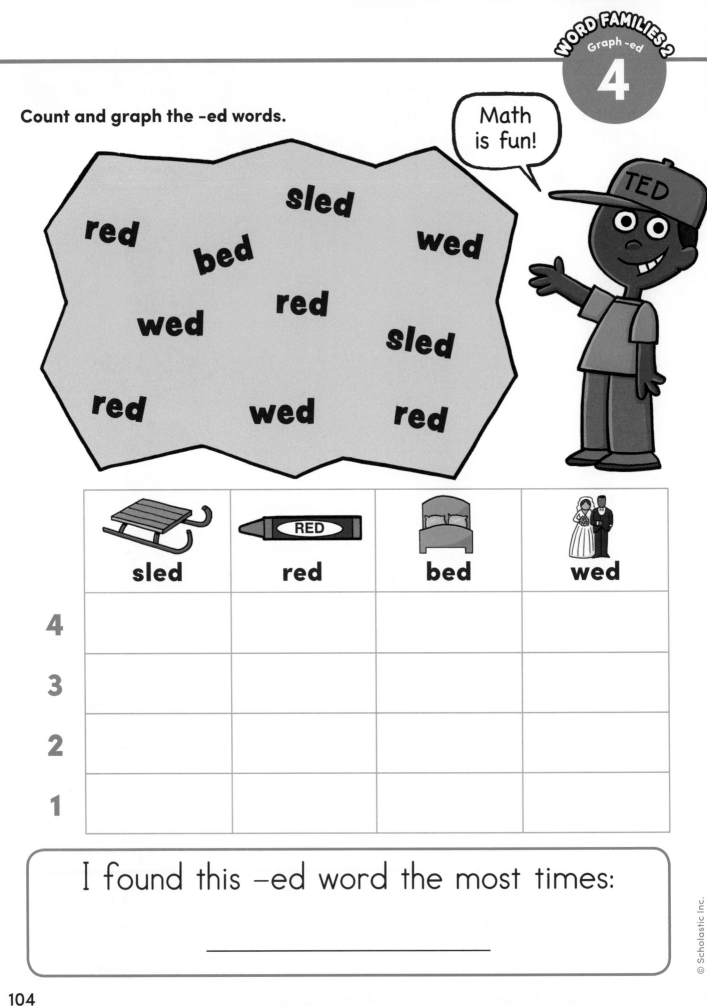 sled	red	bed	wed
4				
3				
2				
1				

I found this –ed word the most times:

_____

© Scholastic Inc.

Read the sentence.
Then write the words.

A girl named **Nell** has a **shell** and a **bell**.

Nell

shell

bell

Use the letters from the letter bank to make more -ell words.

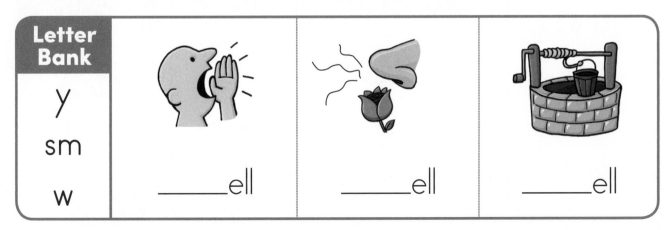

Letter Bank			
y			
sm			
w	____ell	____ell	____ell

© Scholastic Inc.

Match the -ell words to their pictures.

smell •

shell •

yell •

bell •

well •

• (bell)

• (smell)

• (well)

• (shell)

• (yell)

Find each -ell word once.

Word Bank	w e l l n t e
bell	z b e l l u v
shell	q k o y e l l
yell	s h e l l g n
smell	u g s m e l l
well	

You did **swell!**

NELL

© Scholastic Inc.

Count and graph the -ell words.

Math is fun!

NELL

sell

shell

sell

smell

shell

bell

shell

shell

bell

sell

	bell	smell	shell	sell
4				
3				
2				
1				

I found this –ell word the most times:

_____

© Scholastic Inc.

Use each -ed and -ell word once to complete the story. Then read it aloud.

Ted and Nell

His name is _____.

He has a red _____.

Her name is _____.

She has a sea _____

and a big _____.

Where will they keep their stuff?

Inside the _____!

Word Bank	
-ed	**-ell**
shed	bell
Ted	Nell
sled	shell

Great work! Bye!

© Scholastic Inc.

Fill in the -ick and -ing words.

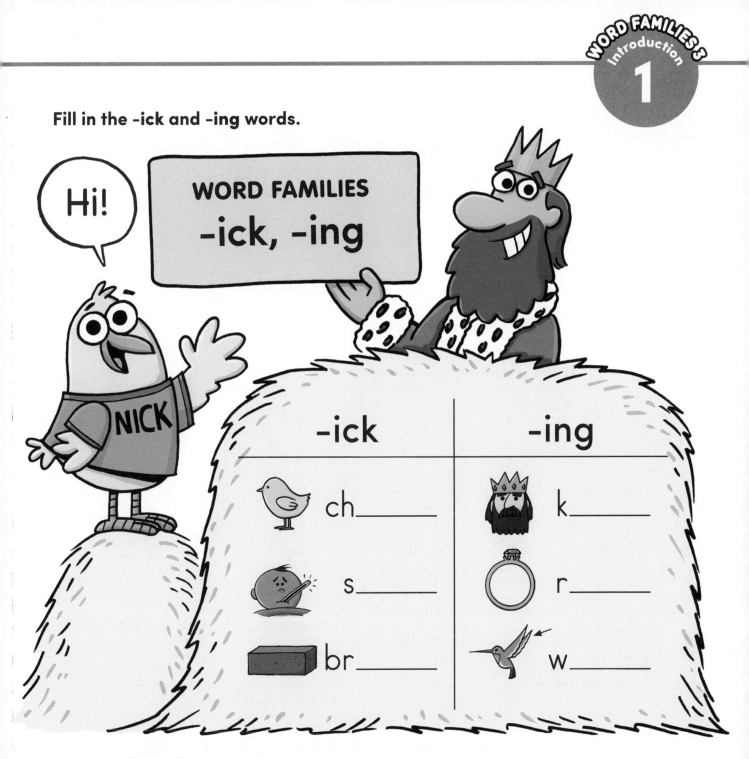

Hi!

WORD FAMILIES
-ick, -ing

NICK

-ick	-ing
ch_____	k_____
s_____	r_____
br_____	w_____

Color in each box when you complete an activity.

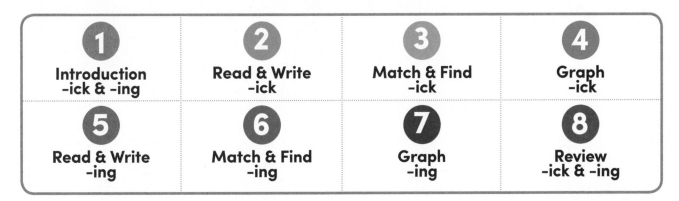

1 Introduction -ick & -ing

2 Read & Write -ick

3 Match & Find -ick

4 Graph -ick

5 Read & Write -ing

6 Match & Find -ing

7 Graph -ing

8 Review -ick & -ing

© Scholastic Inc.

**Read the sentence.
Then write the words.**

"I love to **lick** my lollipop!"
said a **chick** named **Nick**.

lick

chick

Nick

Use the letters from the letter bank to make more -ick words.

Letter Bank			
tr k st	____ick	____ick	____ick

© Scholastic Inc.

Match the -ick words to their pictures.

chick •

stick •

kick •

brick •

sick •

Find each -ick word once.

Word Bank	c a k i c k v
sick	b z c h i c k
stick	s i c k f p e
chick	r s t i c k n
kick	u g b r i c k
brick	

You are **slick**!

NICK

© Scholastic Inc.

Count and graph the -ick words.

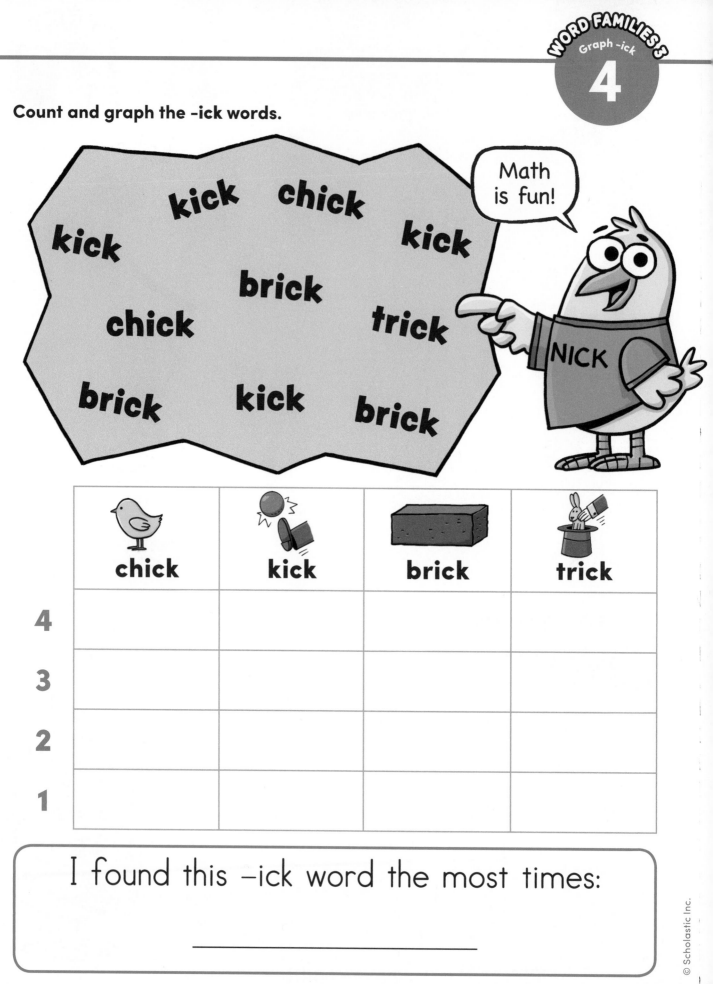

kick chick

kick

kick

brick

chick trick

Math is fun!

NICK

brick kick brick

	chick	kick	brick	trick
4				
3				
2				
1				

I found this –ick word the most times:

_____

© Scholastic Inc.

**Read the sentence.
Then write the words.**

The **king** loves to **swing** in the **spring**.

king ~~king~~

swing ~~swing~~

spring ~~spring~~

Use the letters from the letter bank to make more -ing words.

Letter Bank			
r			
str			
w	_____ing	_____ing	_____ing

© Scholastic Inc.

Match the -ing words to their pictures.

king •

ring •

wing •

sing •

string •

•

Find each -ing word once.

Word Bank						
king	s	c	w	i	n	g	a
ring	s	t	r	i	n	g	n
wing	q	k	o	s	i	n	g
sing	r	k	i	n	g	f	n
string	r	i	n	g	b	o	t

Ding, ding!

© Scholastic Inc.

Count and graph the -ing words.

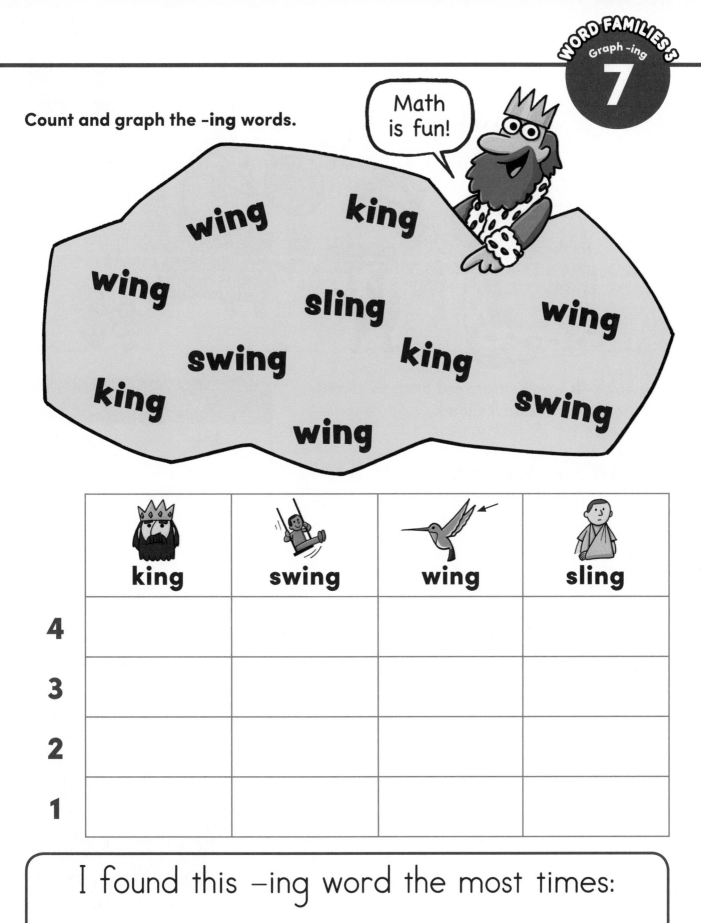

Math is fun!

	king	swing	wing	sling
4				
3				
2				
1				

I found this –ing word the most times:

_____

© Scholastic Inc.

Use each -ick and -ing word once to complete the story. Then read it aloud.

The Chick and the King

Word Bank	
-ick	**-ing**
pick	swing
Nick	ring
chick	spring

Zick, zing!

The season is _____!

The king wears a _____.

The _____ has a lollipop.

His name is _____.

"I will _____ flowers," said the king.

"I will _____," said the chick.

Great work! Bye!

NICK

© Scholastic Inc.

Fill in the -ot and -ock words.

WORD FAMILIES
-ot, -ock

Hi!

-ot	-ock
d_____	cl_____
p_____	s_____
t_____	bl_____

Color in each box when you complete an activity.

1 Introduction -ot & -ock	2 Read & Write -ot	3 Match & Find -ot	4 Graph -ot
5 Read & Write -ock	6 Match & Find -ock	7 Graph -ock	8 Review -ot & -ock

© Scholastic Inc.

**Read the sentence.
Then write the words.**

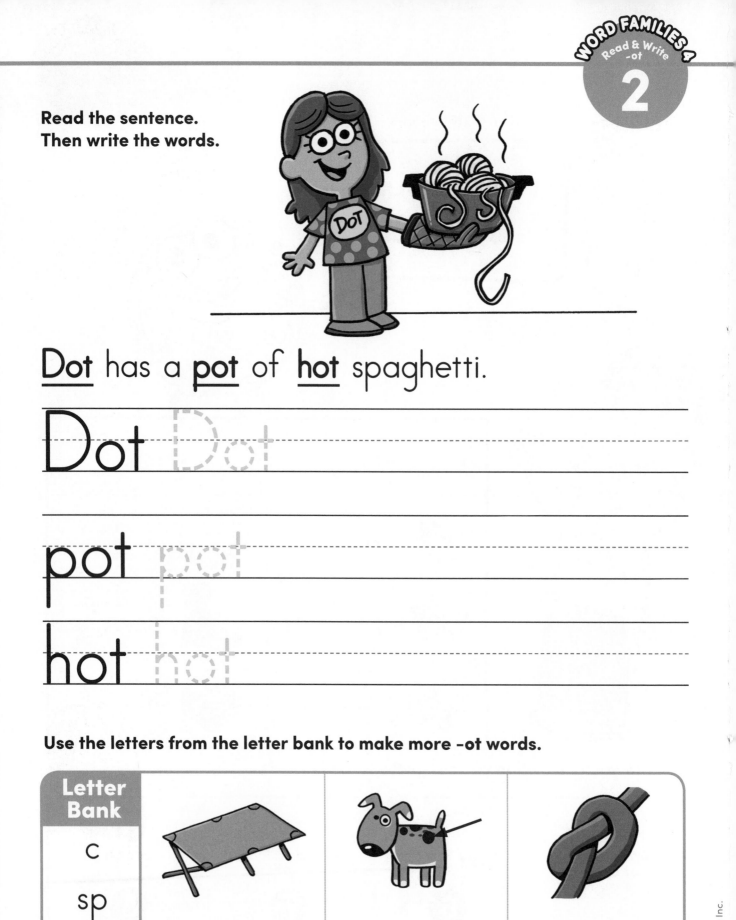

Dot has a **pot** of **hot** spaghetti.

Dot

pot

hot

Use the letters from the letter bank to make more -ot words.

Letter Bank			
c			
sp			
kn	_____ot	_____ot	_____ot

© Scholastic Inc.

Match the -ot words to their pictures.

pot •

hot •

tot •

cot •

spot •

•

•

•

•

•

Find each -ot word once.

You can **spot** the words!

Word Bank	
pot	g c c o t t e
hot	t o t t z u p
tot	j m s p o t e
cot	g h o t g j o
spot	k g v p o t x

© Scholastic Inc.

Count and graph the -ot words.

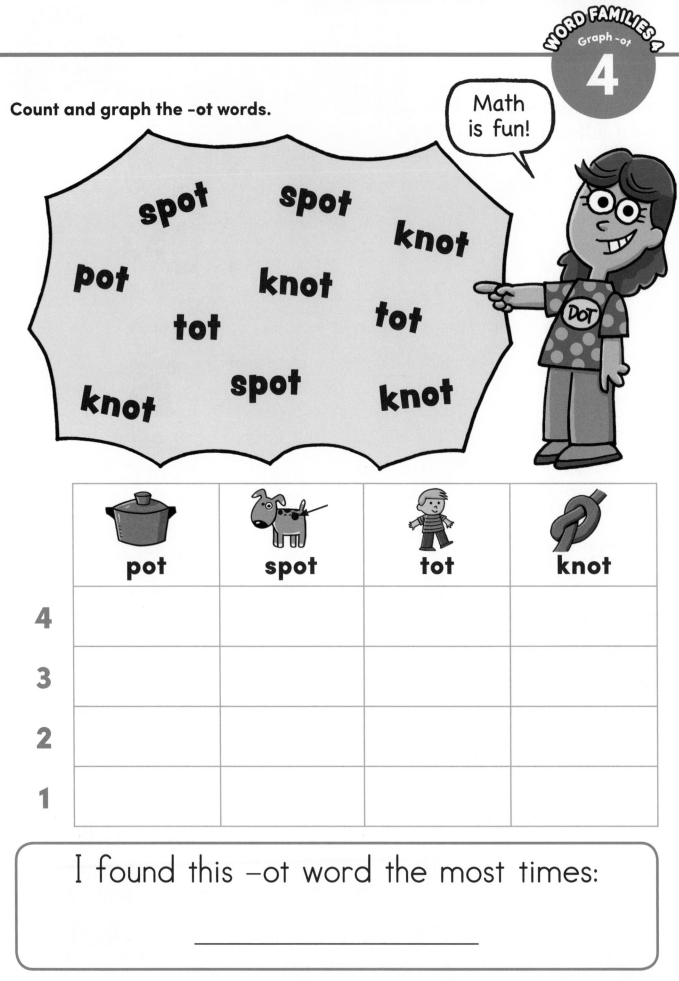

Math is fun!

spot spot knot

pot knot

tot tot

knot spot knot

	pot	spot	tot	knot
4				
3				
2				
1				

I found this –ot word the most times:

_____

© Scholastic Inc.

**Read the sentence.
Then write the words.**

TICK,
TOCK!

The **clock** on the **rock** says, "Tick, **tock**."

clock

rock

tock

Use the letters from the letter bank to make more -ock words.

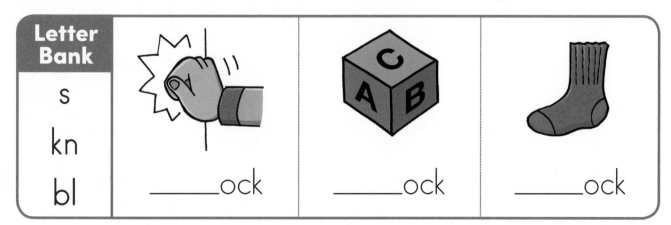

Letter Bank			
s			
kn			
bl	___ock	___ock	___ock

© Scholastic Inc.

Match the -ock words to their pictures.

clock •

rock •

sock •

block •

lock •

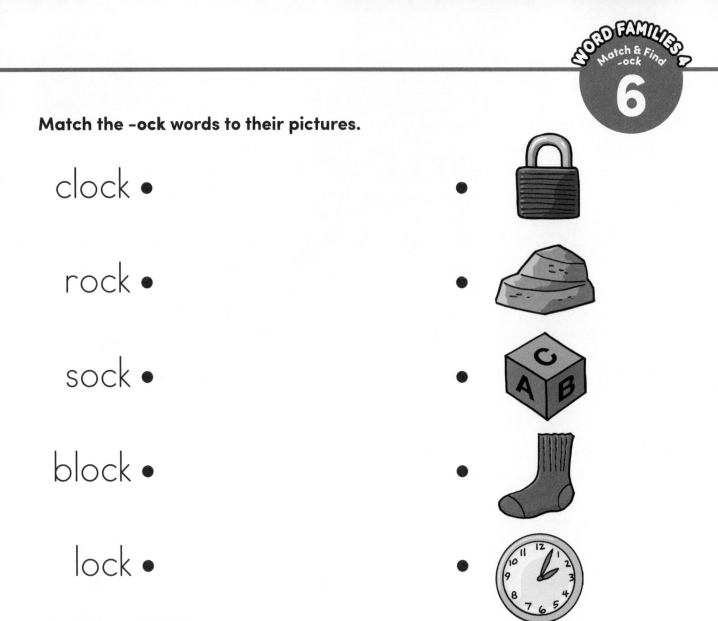

Find each -ock word once.

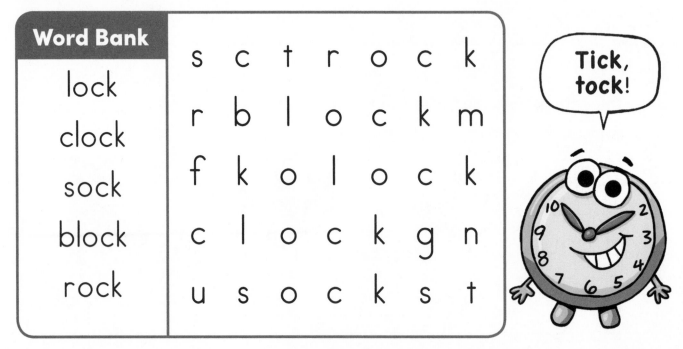

Word Bank						
lock	s	c	t	r	o	c	k
clock	r	b	l	o	c	k	m
sock	f	k	o	l	o	c	k
block	c	l	o	c	k	g	n
rock	u	s	o	c	k	s	t

Tick, tock!

© Scholastic Inc.

Count and graph the -ock words.

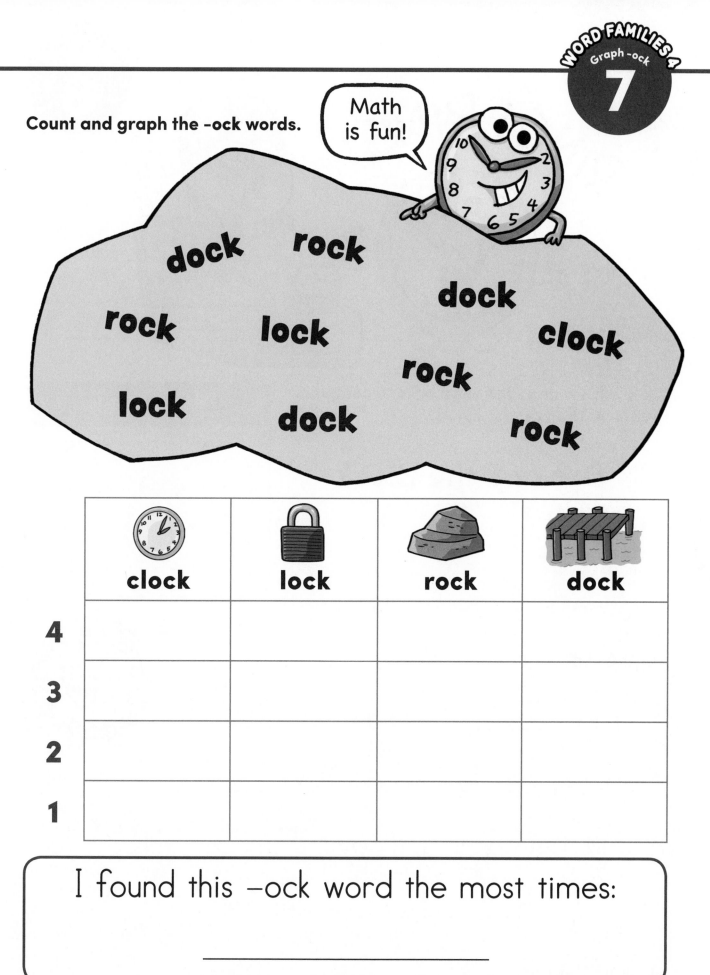

Math is fun!

	![clock]	![lock]	![rock]	![dock]
	clock	**lock**	**rock**	**dock**
4				
3				
2				
1				

I found this –ock word the most times:

_____

© Scholastic Inc.

Use each -ot and -ock word once to complete the story. Then read it aloud.

Dot and the Clock

Word Bank	
-ot	**-ock**
not	rock
Dot	clock
got	tock

_____ has a problem.

She does _____ like to wake up.

So she _____ a new clock.

At night, the clock says, "Tick, _____."

But in the morning, it says, "RING, RING!"

Hooray! The _____ wakes her up.

"Clock, you _____!" says Dot.

© Scholastic Inc.

Fill in the -ug and -uck words.

Hi!

WORD FAMILIES
-ug, -uck

-ug	-uck
b_____	d_____
j_____	b_____
m_____	cl_____

Color in each box when you complete an activity.

1	2	3	4
Introduction -ug & -uck	Read & Write -ug	Match & Find -ug	Graph -ug
5	6	7	8
Read & Write -uck	Match & Find -uck	Graph -uck	Review -ug & -uck

© Scholastic Inc.

Read the sentence.
Then write the words.

A **bug** named **Tug** is in a **mug**.

bug bug

Tug Tug

mug mug

Use the letters from the letter bank to make more -ug words.

Letter Bank			
j pl r	____ug	____ug	____ug

© Scholastic Inc.

Match the -ug words to their pictures.

jug •

rug •

plug •

slug •

mug •

Find each -ug word once.

Word Bank
slug
mug
bug
rug
plug

p l u g l u l
b e s l u g m
q k o p r u g
b u g e x u z
u j s m u g h

Can you find **bug**?

TUG

© Scholastic Inc.

Count and graph the -ug words.

Math is fun!

rug   mug   pug

pug

bug   bug

mug

mug   pug   pug

TUG

	bug	mug	rug	pug
4				
3				
2				
1				

I found this –ug word the most times:

_____

© Scholastic Inc.

**Read the sentence.
Then write the words.**

A **duck** named **Chuck** is in a **truck**!

duck

Chuck

truck

Use the letters from the letter bank to make more -uck words.

Letter Bank			
tr			
r			
b	____uck	____uck	____uck
cl			

© Scholastic Inc.

Match the -uck words to their pictures.

duck •

truck •

buck •

luck •

stuck •

Find each -uck word once.

Word Bank	
buck	y c t b u c k
stuck	l u c k z u m
truck	d u c k f p e
duck	r a s t u c k
luck	t r u c k s t

Good luck!

CHUCK

© Scholastic Inc.

Count and graph the -uck words.

Math is fun!

CHUCK

truck   luck

truck

cluck   duck

duck   duck

duck

luck

truck

	duck	luck	truck	cluck
4				
3				
2				
1				

I found this –uck word the most times:

_____

© Scholastic Inc.

Use each -ug and -uck word once to complete the story. Then read it aloud.

Tug and Chuck

Word Bank	
-ug	**-uck**
mug	duck
jug	Chuck
bug	truck

Tug is a _____.

Chuck is a _____.

Chuck drove his _____

over to see Tug.

Did _____ find Tug

in the _____? No!

Tug was in the _____!

Great work! Bye!

TUG

© Scholastic Inc.

132

Fill in the -am and -ap words.

WORD FAMILIES
-am, -ap

Hi!

-am	-ap
cl_____	c_____
h_____	m_____
sw_____	n_____

Color in each box when you complete an activity.

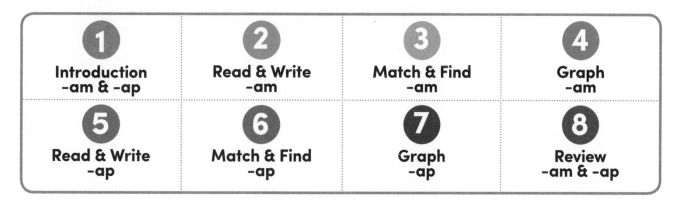

1 Introduction -am & -ap	2 Read & Write -am	3 Match & Find -am	4 Graph -am
5 Read & Write -ap	6 Match & Find -ap	7 Graph -ap	8 Review -am & -ap

© Scholastic Inc.

Read the sentence.
Then write the words.

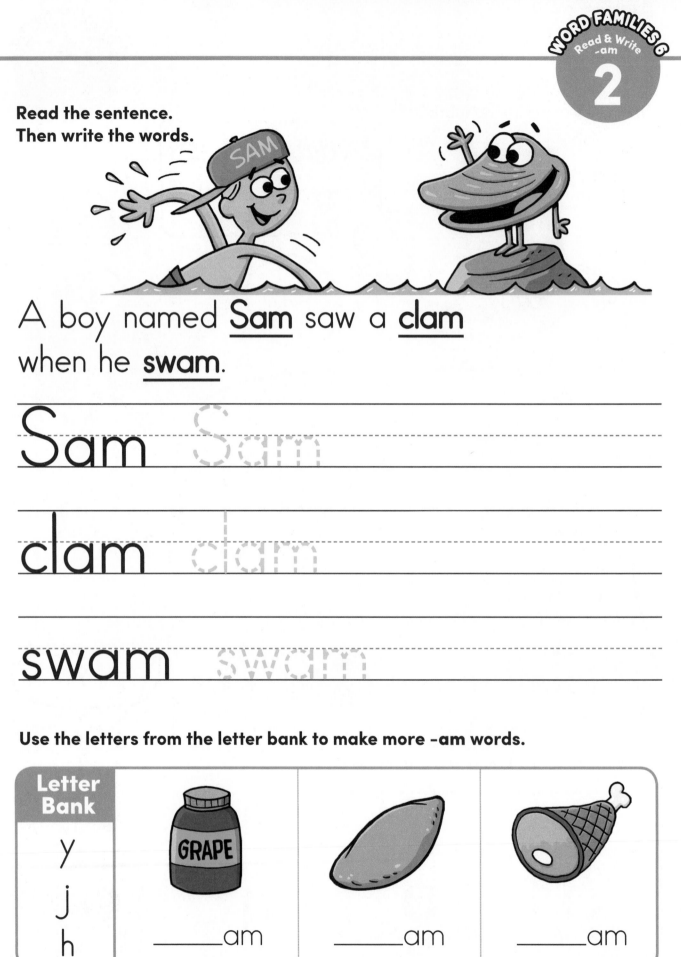

A boy named **Sam** saw a **clam**
when he **swam**.

Sam

clam

swam

Use the letters from the letter bank to make more -am words.

Letter Bank			
y j h	GRAPE ___am	___am	___am

© Scholastic Inc.

Match the -am words to their pictures.

jam •

ham •

ram •

clam •

swam •

Find each -am word once.

Word Bank	
ram	y c h a m t a
swam	b s w a m u m
ham	c l a m f p e
jam	r j a m g g n
clam	u g c b r a m

I **am** proud of you!

© Scholastic Inc.

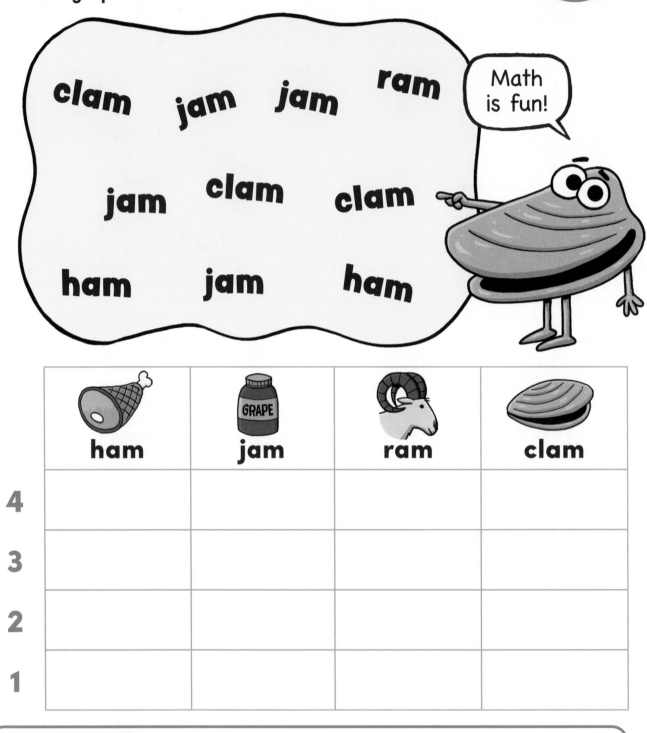

Count and graph the -am words.

clam   jam   jam   ram

Math is fun!

jam   clam   clam

ham   jam   ham

	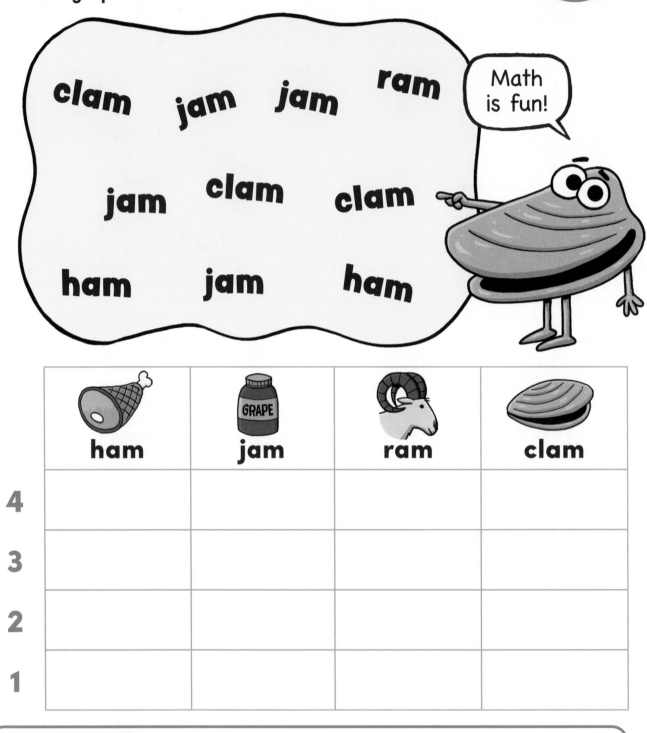ham	jam	ram	clam
4				
3				
2				
1				

I found this –am word the most times:

_____

© Scholastic Inc.

Read the sentence.
Then write the words.

ZZZZZ

MAP

The **cap** with a **map** took a **nap**.

cap

map

nap

Use the letters from the letter bank to make more -ap words.

Letter Bank			
c			
cl			
fl	___ap	___ap	___ap

© Scholastic Inc.

Match the -ap words to their pictures.

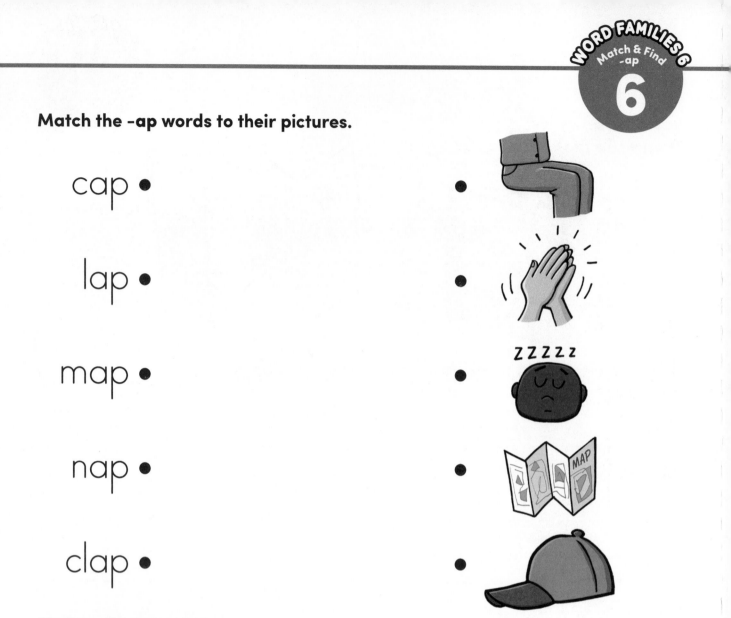

cap •

lap •

map •

nap •

clap •

Find each -ap word once.

Word Bank	
clap	m n r e n a p
map	s f l a p u t
nap	k m a p g z e
lap	c a p e h g n
cap	u g c l a p o

Snap!

© Scholastic Inc.

Count and graph the -ap words.

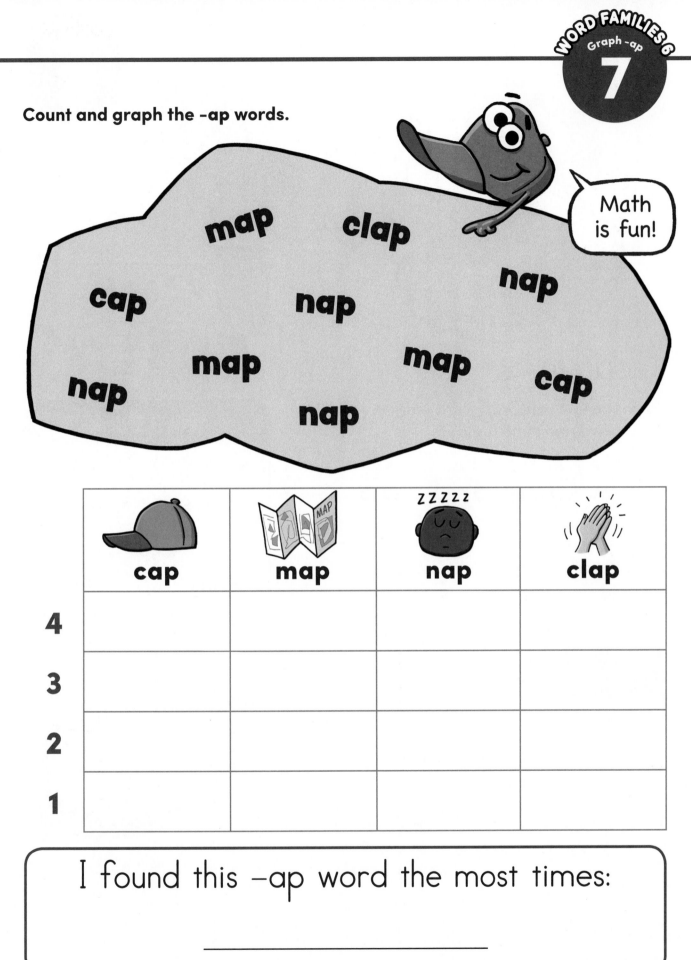

Math is fun!

cap	map	nap	clap
4			
3			
2			
1			

I found this –ap word the most times:

_____

© Scholastic Inc.

Use each -am and -ap word once to complete the story. Then read it aloud.

Clam and Cap

Look at the _____.

It is on the _____!

They have a _____.

They see a dog _____

and a boy named _____.

"I _____ so happy!" said the cap.

"Me, too!" said the clam.

Word Bank

-am	-ap
Sam	nap
clam	map
am	cap

Great work! Bye!

© Scholastic Inc.

140

Fill in the -ill and -ip words.

WORD FAMILIES
-ill, -ip

-ill

-ip

Hi!

h_____

gr_____

sp_____

DIP

d_____

l_____

ch_____

Hi!

JILL

KIP

Color in each box when you complete an activity.

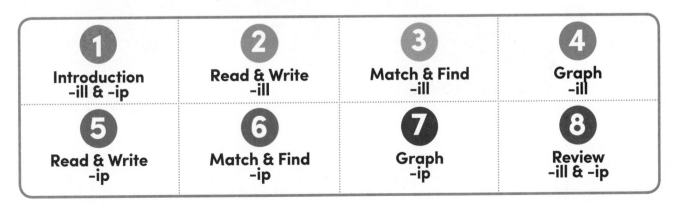

| 1 Introduction -ill & -ip | 2 Read & Write -ill | 3 Match & Find -ill | 4 Graph -ill |
| 5 Read & Write -ip | 6 Match & Find -ip | 7 Graph -ip | 8 Review -ill & -ip |

© Scholastic Inc.

**Read the sentence.
Then write the words.**

<u>J</u>ill <u>will</u> climb up the <u>hill</u>.

Jill

will

hill

Use the letters from the letter bank to make more -ill words.

Letter Bank			
b gr dr	____ill	____ill	____ill

© Scholastic Inc.

Match the -ill words to their pictures.

hill •

bill •

grill •

drill •

quill •

•

Find each -ill word once.

You **will** find all the words!

Word Bank	
drill	d b i l l t a
quill	b e d r i l l
bill	q k o h i l l
hill	r a q u i l l
grill	u g r i l l t

© Scholastic Inc.

Count and graph the -ill words.

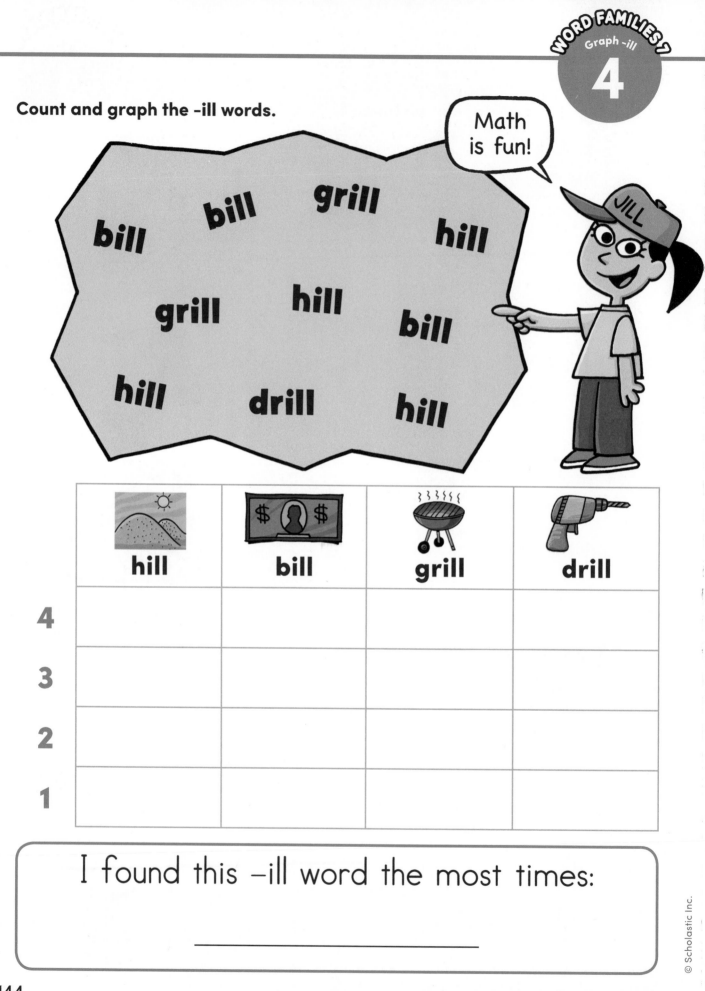

Math
is fun!

	hill	**bill**	**grill**	**drill**
4				
3				
2				
1				

I found this –ill word the most times:

_____

© Scholastic Inc.

Read the sentence.
Then write the words.

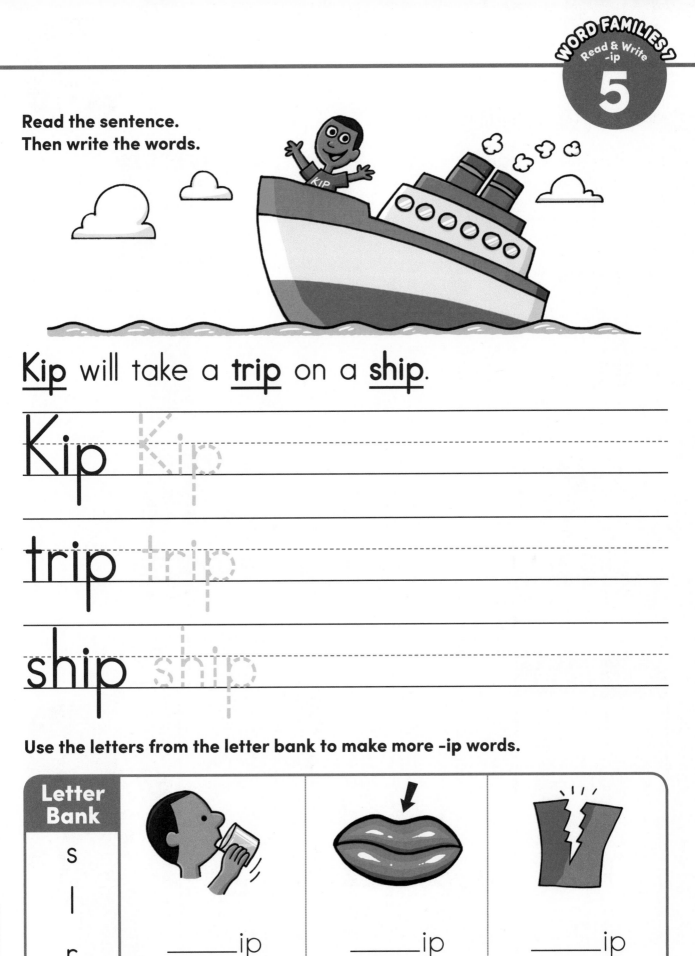

<u>Kip</u> will take a <u>**trip**</u> on a <u>**ship**</u>.

Kip

trip

ship

Use the letters from the letter bank to make more -ip words.

Letter Bank			
s			
l	___ip	___ip	___ip
r			

© Scholastic Inc.

Match the -ip words to their pictures.

lip •

rip •

ship •

hip •

dip •

Find each -ip word once.

Zip zoom!

Word Bank	y c d i p t s
lip	b s h i p u x
dip	l i p d m e q
ship	n a s z r i p
hip	u g c h i p t
rip	

© Scholastic Inc.

Count and graph the -ip words.

Math is fun!

lip	ship	rip	slip
lip	**ship**	**rip**	**slip**

4

3

2

1

I found this –ip word the most times:

_____

© Scholastic Inc.

I **will** be there soon!

JILL

KIP

Use each -ill and -ip word once to complete the story. Then read it aloud.

Jill and Kip

See the sailing _____.

_____ is going to visit Jill.

Jill is on a _____!

"I _____ be there soon," says Kip.

Taking a _____

is such a _____!

Word Bank	
-ill	**-ip**
will	Kip
thrill	ship
hill	trip

Great work! Bye!

KIP

© Scholastic Inc.

Fill in the **-ail** and **-ake** words.

WORD FAMILIES
-ail, -ake

GAIL

Hi!

JAKE

-ail	-ake
sn_____	sn_____
p_____	c_____
m_____	r_____

Color in each box when you complete an activity.

1 Introduction -ail & -ake	**2** Read & Write -ail	**3** Match & Find -ail	**4** Graph -ail
5 Read & Write -ake	**6** Match & Find -ake	**7** Graph -ake	**8** Review -ail & -ake

© Scholastic Inc.

Read the sentence.
Then write the words.

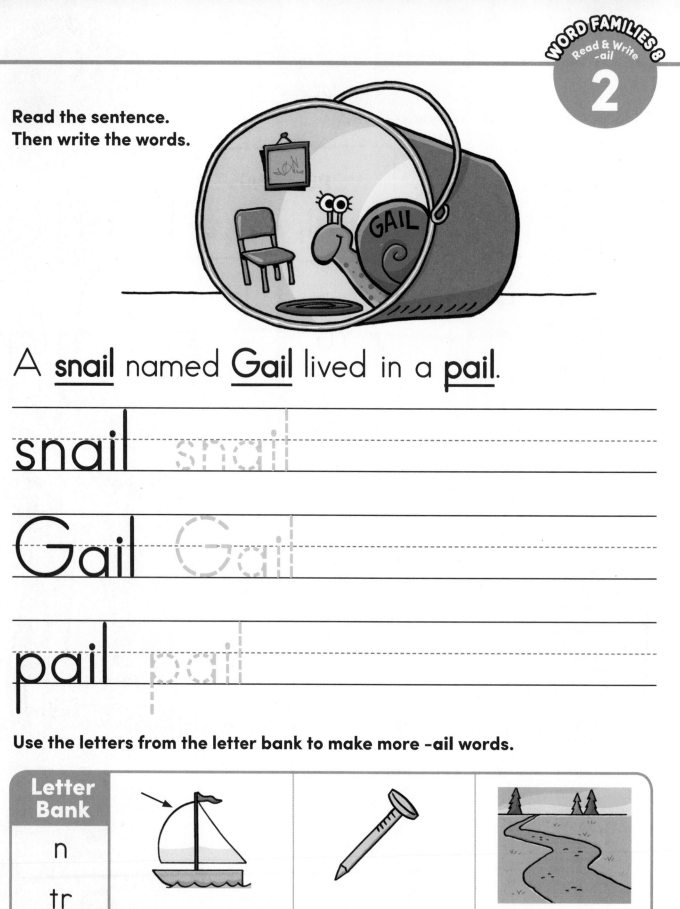

A **snail** named **Gail** lived in a **pail**.

snail

Gail

pail

Use the letters from the letter bank to make more -ail words.

Letter Bank			
n	___ail	___ail	___ail
tr			
s			

© Scholastic Inc.

Match the -ail words to their pictures.

snail •

pail •

tail •

nail •

rail •

Find each -ail word once.

Word Bank
pail
rail
tail
snail
nail

b t a i l t a
n a i l z u g
g k o p a i l
s r a i l g n
u s n a i r r

You will
not **fail!**

GAIL

© Scholastic Inc.

Count and graph the -ail words.

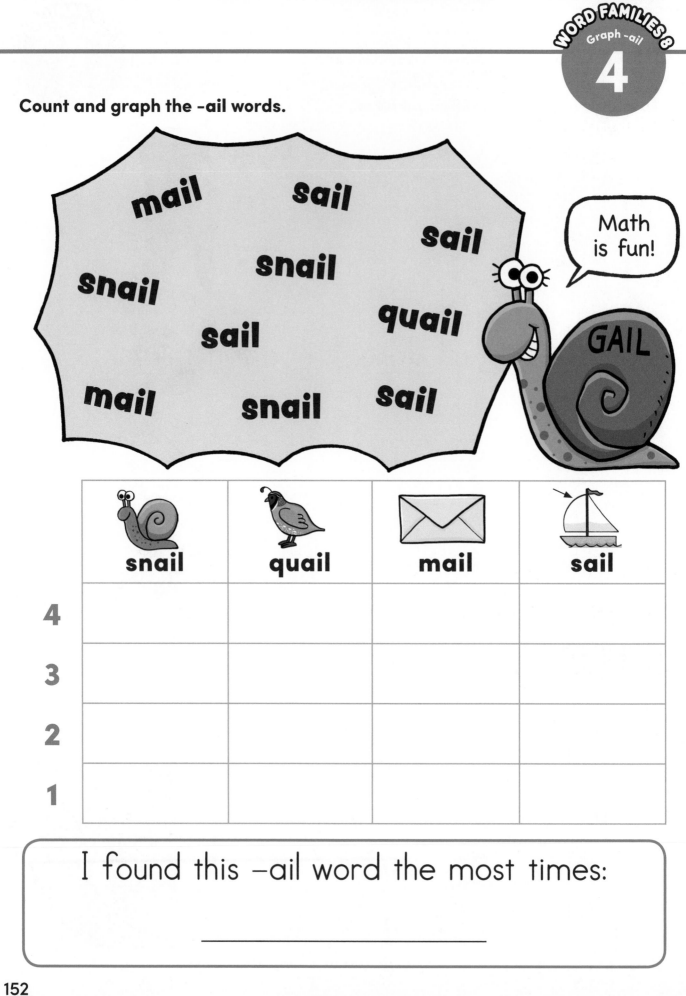

mail   sail

sail

snail

snail

quail

sail

Math is fun!

GAIL

mail   snail   sail

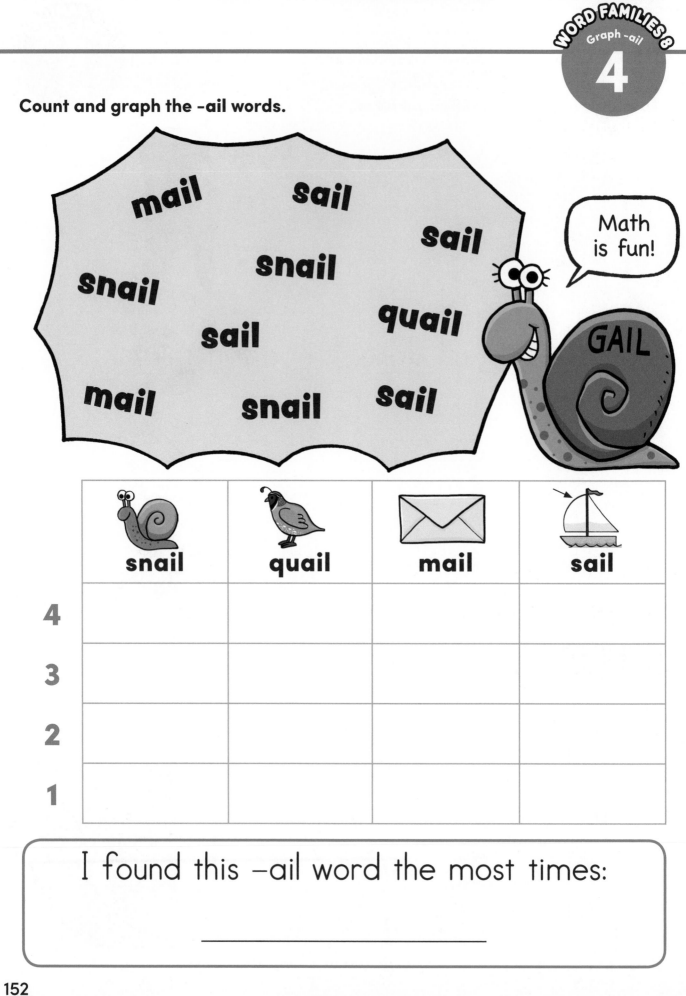 snail	quail	mail	sail

4

3

2

1

I found this –ail word the most times:

_____

© Scholastic Inc.

**Read the sentence.
Then write the words.**

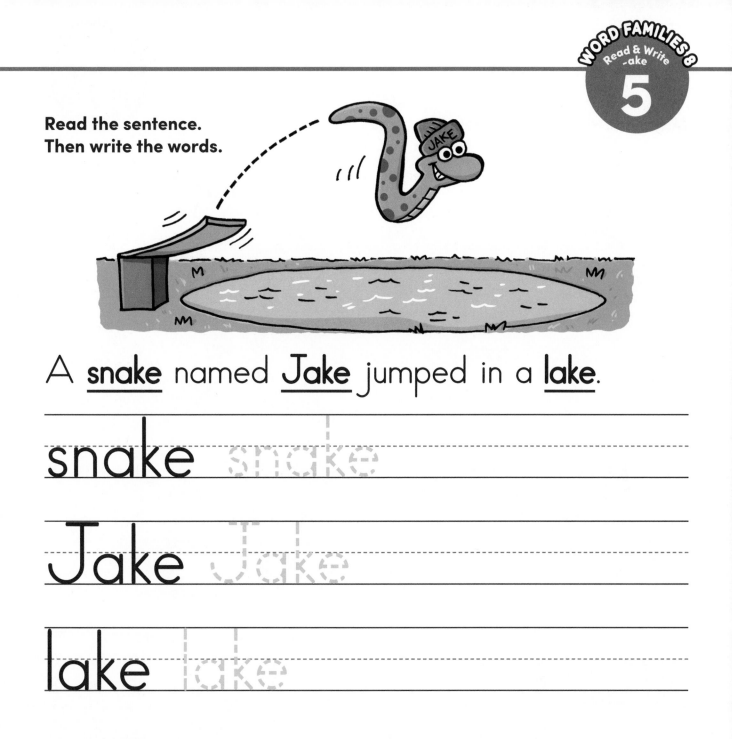

A **snake** named **Jake** jumped in a **lake**.

snake

Jake

lake

Use the letters from the letter bank to make more -ake words.

Letter Bank			
r			
sh	____ake	____ake	____ake
c			

© Scholastic Inc.

153

Match the -ake words to their pictures.

snake •

cake •

lake •

flake •

rake •

Find each -ake word once.

Word Bank	
rake	y c a k e t b
flake	r a k e a u p
cake	s n a k e p r
snake	r a f l a k e
lake	u l a k e s t

Words **make**
me happy!

JAKE

© Scholastic Inc.

Count and graph the -ake words.

Math is fun!

 snake	lake	shake	cake
4			
3			
2			
1			

I found this —ake word the most times:

_____

© Scholastic Inc.

155

Use each -ail and -ake word once to complete the story. Then read it aloud.

Gail and Jake

Word Bank	
-ail	**-ake**
pail	Jake
trail	snake
snail	cake

Gail is a _____.

Jake is a _____.

Look! Jake baked a _____!

Then he slid along a _____.

When he got to Gail's _____,

_____ sang, "Happy Birthday to you!"

Great work! Bye!

© Scholastic Inc.

Fill in the -ee and -eep words.

Hi!

WORD FAMILIES
-ee, -eep

-ee	-eep
b_____	sh_____
thr_____	j_____
tr_____	sw_____

Color in each box when you complete an activity.

1 Introduction -ee & -eep	**2** Read & Write -ee	**3** Match & Find -ee	**4** Graph -ee
5 Read & Write -eep	**6** Match & Find -eep	**7** Graph -eep	**8** Review -ee & -eep

© Scholastic Inc.

**Read the sentence.
Then write the words.**

Can you **see** the **bee** hiding in the **tree**?

see ~~see~~

bee ~~bee~~

tree ~~tree~~

Use the letters from the letter bank to make more -ee words.

Letter Bank			
gl thr kn	____ee	____ee	____ee

© Scholastic Inc.

Match the -ee words to their pictures.

bee •

tree •

knee •

three •

glee •

•

Find each -ee word once.

Word Bank							
three	k	c	t	r	e	e	a
bee	b	e	e	t	z	u	m
tree	q	t	h	r	e	e	p
glee	r	h	k	n	e	e	n
knee	u	g	l	e	e	s	r

I am filled with **glee**!

© Scholastic Inc.

Count and graph the -ee words.

knee   see

bee   bee

bee

knee   see

three   see   bee

Math is fun!

bee	see	knee	three

4

3

2

1

I found this -ee word the most times:

_____

© Scholastic Inc.

Read the sentence.
Then write the words.

BEEP! BEEP!

The **sheep** is in a **jeep**. Beep, **beep**!

sheep

jeep

beep

Use the letters from the letter bank to make more -eep words.

Letter Bank			
p	peep		
s w			
s l	___eep	___eep	___eep

© Scholastic Inc.

Match the -eep words to their pictures.

sheep •

jeep •

sleep •

sweep •

peep •

peep

Find each -eep word once.

Word Bank							
jeep sheep peep sleep sweep	y	c	p	e	e	p	a
	s	g	s	w	e	e	p
	q	s	h	e	e	p	n
	j	e	e	p	g	t	y
	u	s	l	e	e	p	t

Keep up the
great work!

162

© Scholastic Inc.

Count and graph the -eep words.

Math is fun!

sleep sweep

sleep sheep sweep

sweep sweep

sheep sleep jeep

	![sheep] sheep	![jeep] jeep	![sweep] sweep	![sleep] sleep
4				
3				
2				
1				

I found this –eep word the most times:

_____

© Scholastic Inc.

Use each -ee and -eep word once to complete the story. Then read it aloud.

Bee and Sheep

See the striped _____!

See the white _____!

They are in a _____.

They _____ two birds

and _____ big bears.

Beep, _____!

Word Bank	
-ee	**-eep**
see	beep
bee	sheep
three	jeep

Great work! Bye!

© Scholastic Inc.

Fill in the -ice and -ight words.

WORD FAMILIES
-ice, -ight

Hi!

-ice	-ight
m_____	kn_____
_____	l_____
d_____	f_____

Color in each box when you complete an activity.

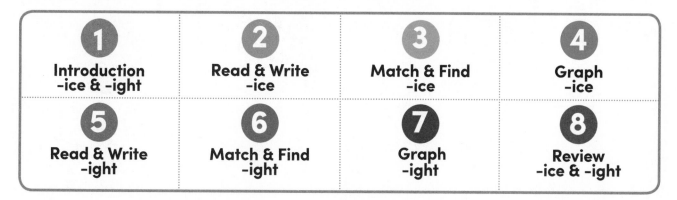

1 Introduction -ice & -ight	**2** Read & Write -ice	**3** Match & Find -ice	**4** Graph -ice
5 Read & Write -ight	**6** Match & Find -ight	**7** Graph -ight	**8** Review -ice & -ight

© Scholastic Inc.

Read the sentence.
Then write the words.

The **nice** **mice** eat a bowl of **ice** cream.

nice nice

mice mice

ice ice

Use the letters from the letter bank to make more -ice words.

Letter Bank			
r			
d	___ice	___ice	___ice
s l			

© Scholastic Inc.

Match the -ice words to their pictures.

mice •

ice •

rice •

slice •

dice •

Find each -ice word once.

Word Bank	
slice	g c m i c e h
dice	b e d i c e m
rice	i c e p f k j
ice	r a s l i c e
mice	u g c r i c e

Words are **nice!**

© Scholastic Inc.

Count and graph the -ice words.

Math is fun!

ice

slice

rice

slice

mice

mice

slice

rice

rice

rice

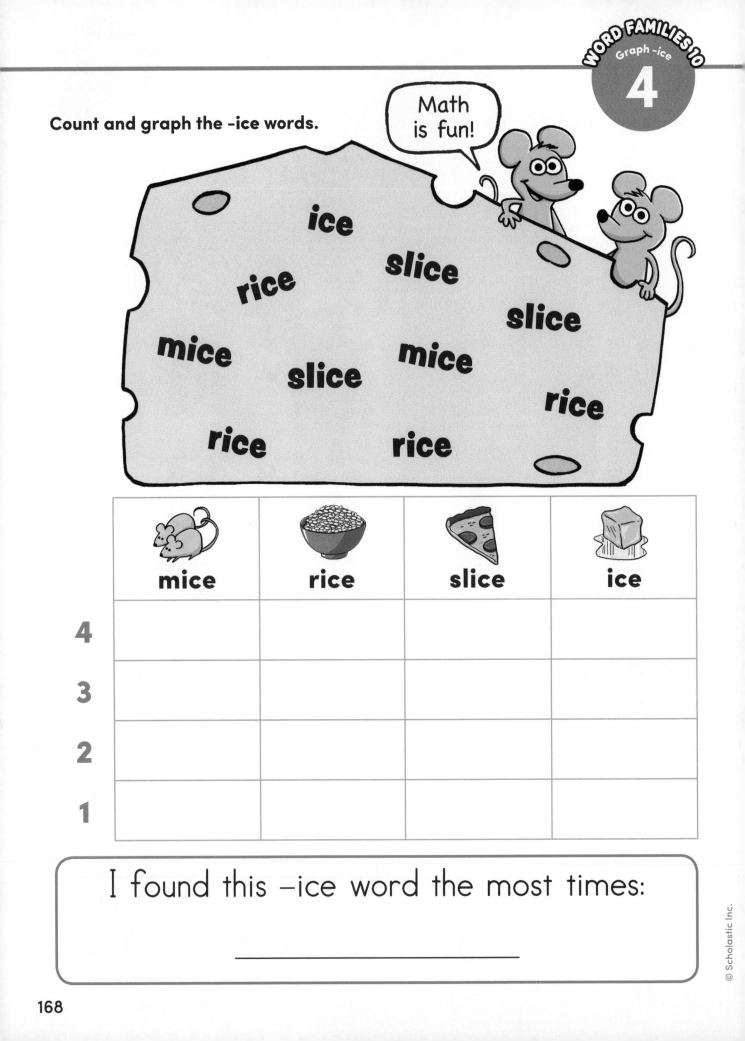 mice	rice	slice	ice
4			
3			
2			
1			

I found this –ice word the most times:

_____

© Scholastic Inc.

Read the sentence.
Then write the words.

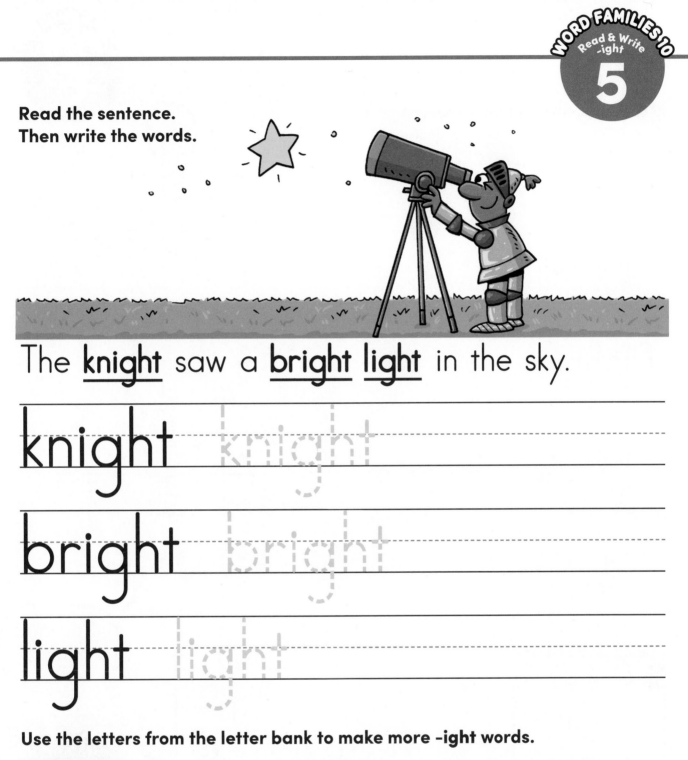

The **knight** saw a **bright light** in the sky.

knight

bright

light

Use the letters from the letter bank to make more -ight words.

Letter Bank			
n			
fl	___ight	___ight	___ight
r			

© Scholastic Inc.

Match the -ight words to their pictures.

knight •

light •

flight •

fight •

right •

• (lightbulb)

• (airplane)

• (arrow)

• (knight)

• (fight)

You are **right!**

Find each -ight word once.

Word Bank						
right	f	i	g	h	t	r	a
knight	f	l	i	g	h	t	d
fight	q	k	r	i	g	h	t
flight	r	o	l	i	g	h	t
light	k	n	i	g	h	t	z

© Scholastic Inc.

Count and graph the –ight words.

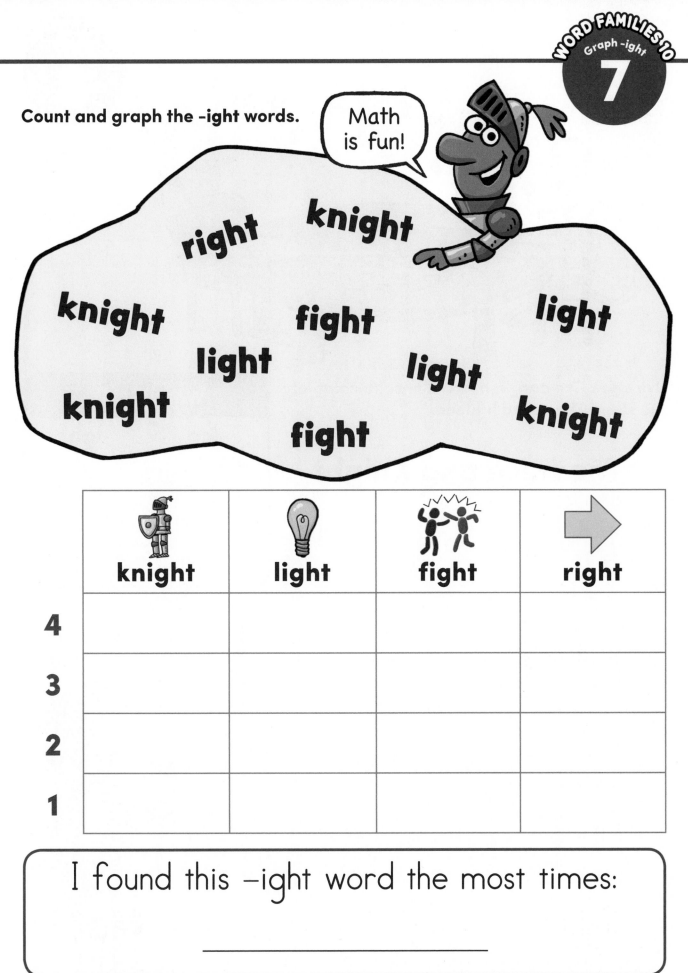

Math is fun!

knight	light	fight	right

4

3

2

1

I found this –ight word the most times:

_____

© Scholastic Inc.

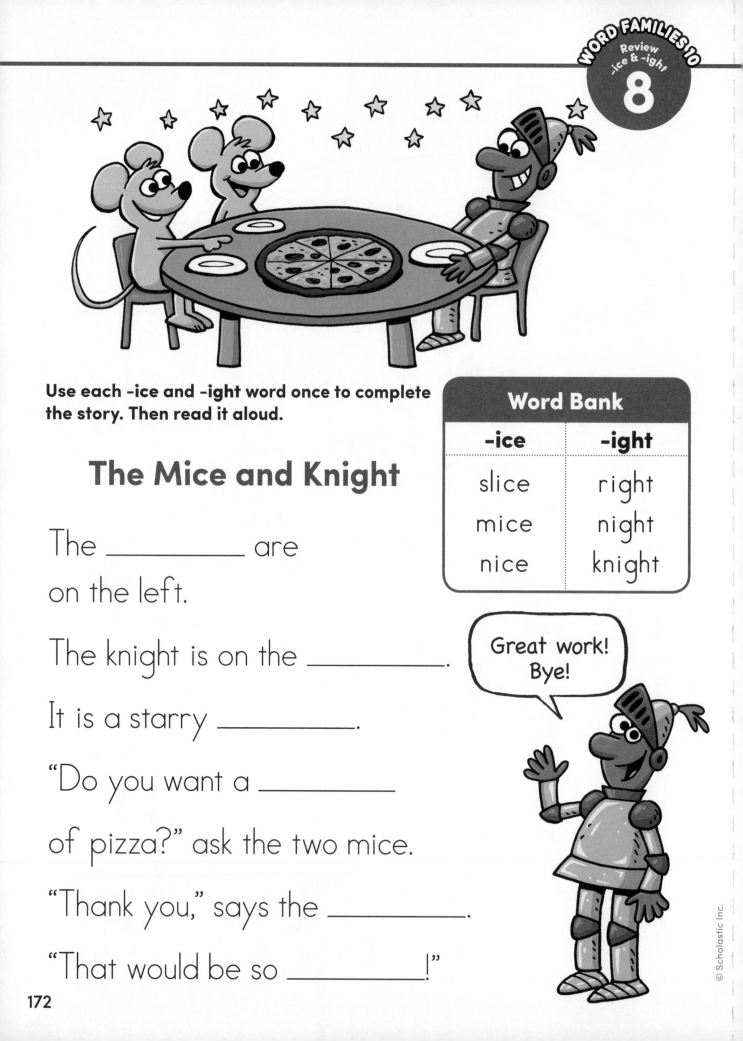

Use each -ice and -ight word once to complete the story. Then read it aloud.

The Mice and Knight

Word Bank	
-ice	**-ight**
slice	right
mice	night
nice	knight

The _____ are
on the left.

The knight is on the _____.

It is a starry _____.

"Do you want a _____

of pizza?" ask the two mice.

"Thank you," says the _____.

"That would be so _____!"

Great work! Bye!

© Scholastic Inc.

172

Family Activities

Here are some skill-building activities that you and your child might enjoy.

Sidewalk Chalkboard

Your child may find practicing spelling words or handwriting more like play when using colorful sidewalk chalk outdoors. Challenge your child to write words as big as possible, then as small as possible.

Sight Word Search

While flipping through a magazine, encourage your child to look for sight words, such as *the, of, to, you, she, my, is, are, do*, and *does*. Have your child say and circle the words. Then have your child count how many of each word he or she found on a page or in an article.

Word of the Day

Make a list of sight words, such as *the, to, and, a, he, I, you, it, of, in, was, said, that, she, for*, and so on. Pick a word of the day and have your child point out that word every time he or she sees it.

Sighting Sight Words

When reading with your child, point to sight words such as *the, of, to, you, she, my, is, are, do*, and *does*. Say the word and have your child repeat after you. Then point to the word again and have your child say it and use it in a sentence.

SIGHT WORDS
is, a, of, in

Hi!

is   is

a   a

of   of

in   in

Write the words above. Color in each box when you complete an activity.

1 Introduction	2 Read & Write	3 Read & Write	4 Color
5 Graph	6 Match & Find	7 Unscramble	8 Review

© Scholastic Inc.

Read the sentence.

The monster **is** playing with **a** friend.

Write the sight words.

is

a

176

© Scholastic Inc.

Read the sentence.

There are lots **of** socks **in** the monster soup.

Write the sight words.

of

in

© Scholastic Inc.

Use the code to color the sight words.

is → red

of → yellow

a → blue

in → green

Zzzz

is	of	is	of
a	in	a	in
is	of	is	of
a	in	a	in

© Scholastic Inc.

Count and graph the sight words.

	is	a	of	in
4				
3				
2				
1				

© Scholastic Inc.

Draw lines to match the sight words.

is •   • in

a •   • of

of •   • a

in •   • is

in •   • a

of •   • in

is •   • is

a •   • of

Circle each sight word from the Word Bank once.

h g a d x q u m

p b i s u c w v

c g z e k r o f

k u g i n v f w

Word Bank

is a of in

180

© Scholastic Inc.

Unscramble each sight word.

is   a   of   in

fo _____

a _____

si _____

a _____

fo _____

ni _____

si _____

ni _____

© Scholastic Inc.

Word Bank

is

a

of

in

Use each sight word once to complete the story. Then read it aloud.

Here is _____ monster.

He has a bowl _____ soup.

He is _____ a house with a pal.

He _____ so happy.

Bye! Great work!

Color the boxes with the four sight words you learned in this set.

is	we	the	of
you	a	in	to

© Scholastic Inc.

SIGHT WORDS
and, the, to, you

Hi!

and
the
to
you

Write the words above. Color in each box when you complete an activity.

1 Introduction	**2** Read & Write	**3** Read & Write	**4** Color
5 Graph	**6** Match & Find	**7** Unscramble	**8** Review

© Scholastic Inc.

Read the sentence.

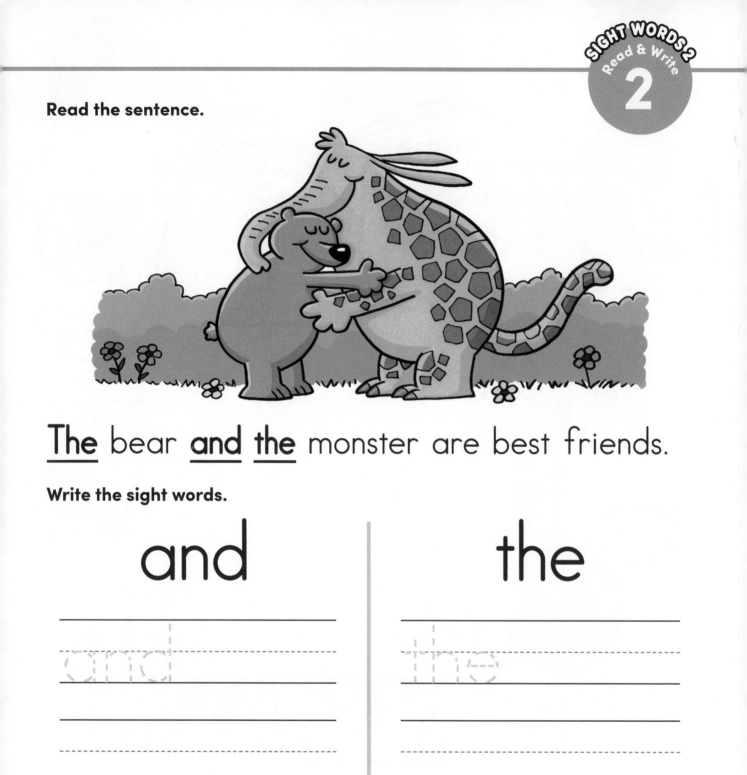

<u>**The**</u> bear <u>**and**</u> <u>**the**</u> monster are best friends.

Write the sight words.

and

~~and~~

- - - - - - - - - - - - - - -

- - - - - - - - - - - - - - -

- - - - - - - - - - - - - - -
----

the

~~the~~

- - - - - - - - - - - - - - -

- - - - - - - - - - - - - - -

- - - - - - - - - - - - - - -

© Scholastic Inc.

Read the sentence.

"I have a gift **<u>to</u>** give **<u>you</u>**!" said the monster.

Write the sight words.

to

you

© Scholastic Inc.

Use the code to color the sight words.

and — red
to — yellow

the — blue
you — green

Zzzz

and	the	you	the
to	and	to	you
and	the	and	you
to	you	to	the

© Scholastic Inc.

Count and graph the sight words.

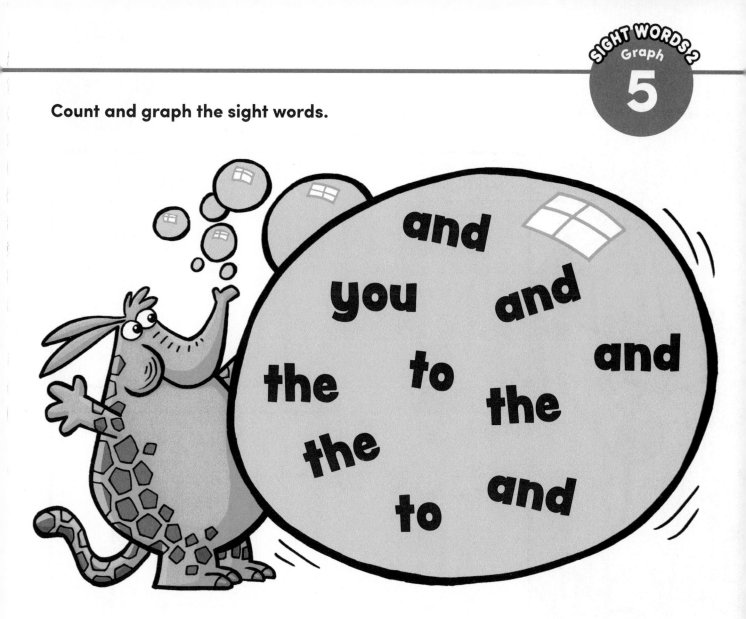

	and	**the**	**to**	**you**
4				
3				
2				
1				

© Scholastic Inc.

Draw lines to match the sight words.

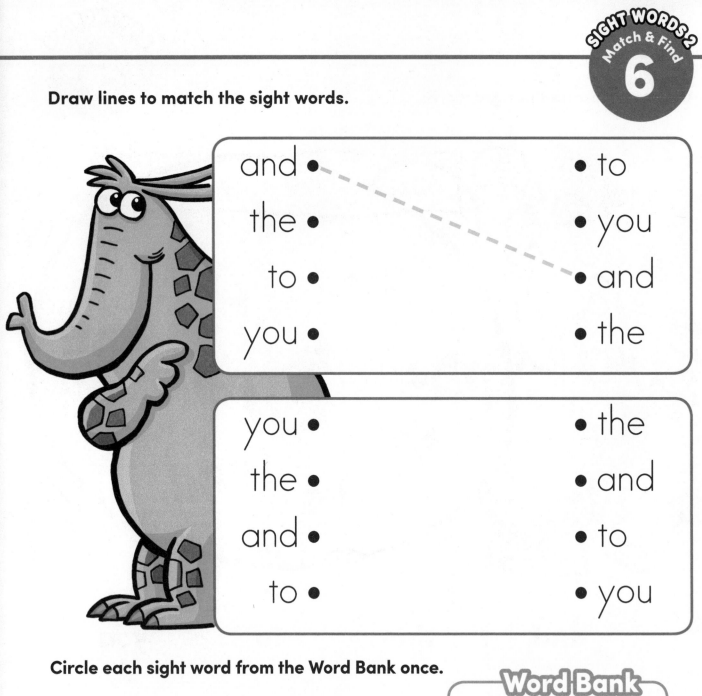

and •   • to

the •   • you

to •   • and

you •   • the

you •   • the

the •   • and

and •   • to

to •   • you

Circle each sight word from the Word Bank once.

p d t h e g w a

f y z e t o s f

n c y o u x p t

n x a n d v i p

Word Bank

and   the
to   you

Unscramble each sight word.

and the to you

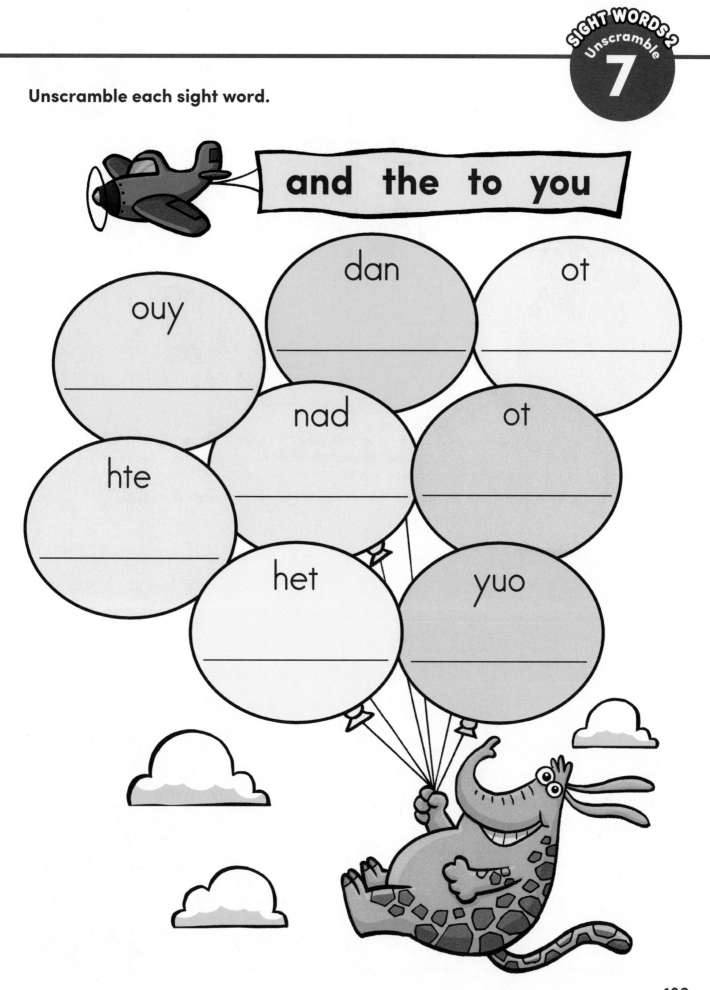

ouy

_____

dan

_____

ot

_____

hte

_____

nad

_____

ot

_____

het

_____

yuo

_____

Word Bank

and

the

to

you

Use each sight word once to complete the story. Then read it aloud.

See the monster _____ the bear.

They went _____ the park.

The monster is on _____ swing.

"Will _____ push me?" he asked the bear.

Color the boxes with the four sight words you learned in this set.

and	or	the	be
I	to	he	you

BYE!
GREAT
WORK!

© Scholastic Inc.

SIGHT WORDS
that, it, he, was

Hi!

that
it
he
was

Write the words above. Color in each box when you complete an activity.

1 Introduction	2 Read & Write	3 Read & Write	4 Color
5 Graph	6 Match & Find	7 Unscramble	8 Review

© Scholastic Inc.

Read the sentence.

The monster was sad **that** **it** was raining.

Write the sight words.

that

it

© Scholastic Inc.

Read the sentence.

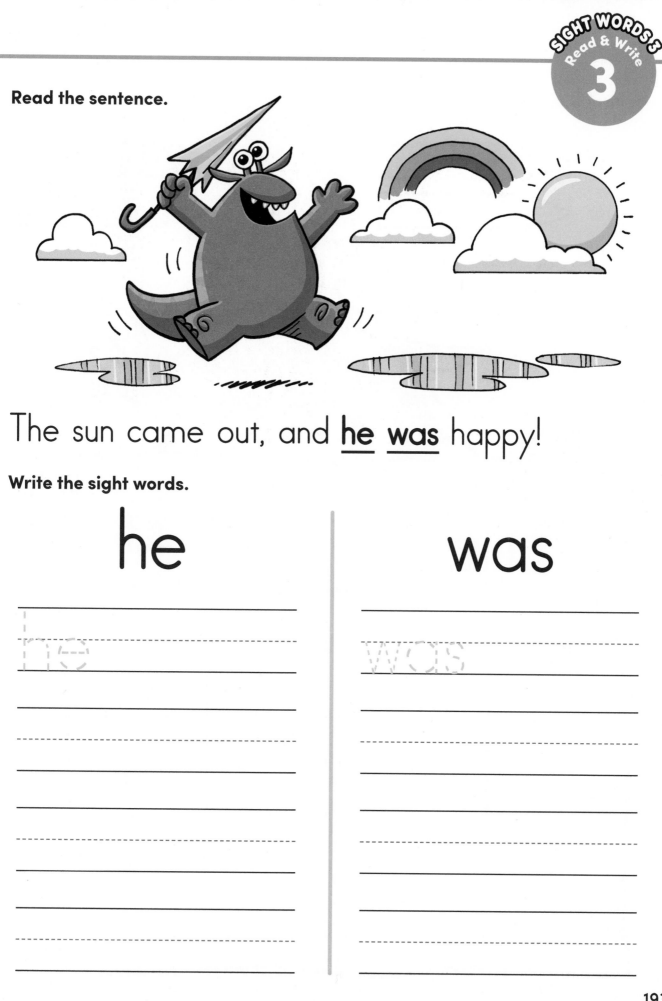

The sun came out, and **he** **was** happy!

Write the sight words.

he

was

© Scholastic Inc.

Use the code to color the sight words.

that → red

he → yellow

it → blue

was → green

Z zZz

he	was	he	was
that	it	was	it
he	was	it	that
that	he	that	it

© Scholastic Inc.

Count and graph the sight words.

	that	it	he	was
4				
3				
2				
1				

© Scholastic Inc.

Draw lines to match the sight words.

that •   • was
it •   • he
he •   • it
was •   • that

that •   • was
it •   • he
he •   • it
was •   • that

Circle each sight word from the Word Bank once.

z p x w a s o d

u r h e c f p w

d g y i t n j v

o t h a t g k j

Word Bank

that it
he was

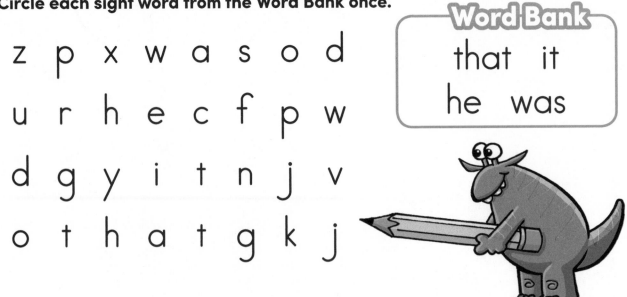

© Scholastic Inc.

Unscramble each sight word.

that   it   he   was

hatt

_____

ti

_____

eh

_____

saw

_____

aws

_____

eh

_____

atth

_____

ti

_____

© Scholastic Inc.

Use each sight word once to complete the story. Then read it aloud.

The monster _____ at the beach.

He saw _____ big fish.

He saw _____ jump up and wave.

So _____ said, "Hello, big fish!"

**Color the boxes with the four sight words
you learned in this set.**

not	it	the	that
was	he	can	said

© Scholastic Inc.

Hi!

SIGHT WORDS
she, for, are, as

she   she

for   for

are   are

as   as

Write the words above. Color in each box when you complete an activity.

1	2	3	4
Introduction	**Read & Write**	**Read & Write**	**Color**
5	6	7	8
Graph	**Match & Find**	**Unscramble**	**Review**

© Scholastic Inc.

Read the sentence.

Look, **she** has a teddy bear **for** the baby!

Write the sight words.

she

for

© Scholastic Inc.

Read the sentence.

The cats **are** **as** sleepy **as** the baby monster.

Write the sight words.

are

as

© Scholastic Inc.

Use the code to color the sight words.

she — red
are — yellow

for — blue
as — green

Zzzz

are	as	for	as
she	for	she	are
she	are	as	as
are	for	she	for

© Scholastic Inc.

Count and graph the sight words.

	she	for	are	as
4				
3				
2				
1				

© Scholastic Inc.

Draw lines to match the sight words.

she •   • for

for •   • as

are •   • are

as •   • she

as •   • as

are •   • for

for •   • she

she •   • are

Circle each sight word from the Word Bank once.

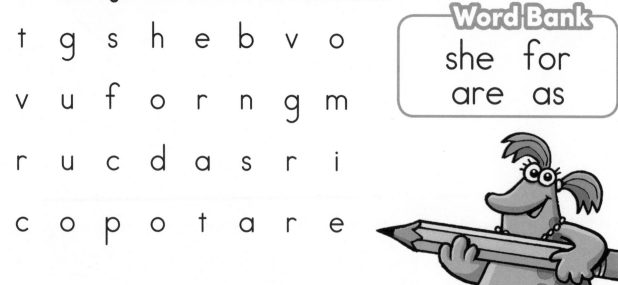

t g s h e b v o

v u f o r n g m

r u c d a s r i

c o p o t a r e

Word Bank

she for

are as

© Scholastic Inc.

Unscramble each sight word.

she   for   are   as

orf _____

sa _____

hes _____

seh _____

rae _____

ear _____

sa _____

rof _____

© Scholastic Inc.

she

for

are

as

Use each sight word once to complete the story. Then read it aloud.

Here _____ two nice monsters.

He is a baby, and _____ is a mom.

She has a bottle _____ the baby.

He is _____ happy as can be!

BYE! GREAT JOB!

Color the boxes with the four sight words you learned in this set.

a	for	by	are
is	as	said	she

© Scholastic Inc.

Write the words above. Color in each box when you complete an activity.

1 Introduction	**2** Read & Write	**3** Read & Write	**4** Color
5 Graph	**6** Match & Find	**7** Unscramble	**8** Review

© Scholastic Inc.

Read the sentence.

"I am **on** top of the mountain!" said the monster.

Write the sight words.

I

on

© Scholastic Inc.

Read the sentence.

"I am happy **they** are here **with** me!"
said the monster.

Write the sight words.

they

with

© Scholastic Inc.

Use the code to color the sight words.

I — red
they — yellow

on — blue
with — green

Zzzz

with	they	I	they
they	I	on	I
I	on	with	they
on	with	on	with

© Scholastic Inc.

Count and graph the sight words.

	I	on	they	with
4				
3				
2				
1				

© Scholastic Inc.

Draw lines to match the sight words.

I •   • on

on •   • with

they •   • they

with •   • I

with •   • on

on •   • I

I •   • with

they •   • they

Circle each sight word from the Word Bank once.

b w I t h p a c

s a t h e y u w

h I x o n y a v

b c a l w i t h

Word Bank

I   on
they   with

© Scholastic Inc.

Unscramble each sight word.

I on they with

I

____

no

____

yeth

____

thiw

____

no

____

hiwt

____

ethy

____

I

____

© Scholastic Inc.

213

I
on
they
with

Use each sight word once to complete the story. Then read it aloud.

The pals put _____ their skates.

Then _____ skated on the lake.

"_____ like to skate with you!"

said the monster.

"We like to skate _____ you, too!"

said the penguins.

Color the boxes with the four sight words you learned in this set.

I	said	a	with
all	on	they	he

BYE!
GREAT
JOB!

© Scholastic Inc.

SIGHT WORDS
be, at, have, this

Hi!

be — be
at — at
have — have
this — this

Write the words above. Color in each box when you complete an activity.

1 Introduction	2 Read & Write	3 Read & Write	4 Color
5 Graph	6 Match & Find	7 Unscramble	8 Review

© Scholastic Inc.

Read the sentence.

The monster loves to **be at** the hat shop!

Write the sight words.

be

at

© Scholastic Inc.

Read the sentence.

"I **have** to try on **this** tall hat!" said the monster.

Write the sight words.

have

this

© Scholastic Inc.

Use the code to color the sight words.

be — red

have — yellow

at — blue

this — green

have	this	have	this
be	at	at	be
have	this	at	have
be	at	be	this

© Scholastic Inc.

Count and graph the sight words.

	be	at	have	this
4				
3				
2				
1				

© Scholastic Inc.

Draw lines to match the sight words.

be •   • have

at •   • this

have •   • be

this •   • at

at •   • this

have •   • at

be •   • be

this •   • have

Circle each sight word from the Word Bank once.

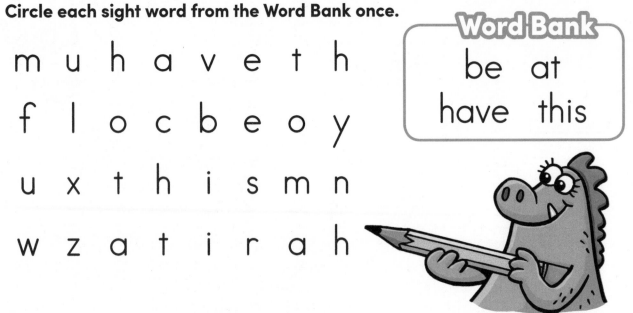

m u h a v e t h

f l o c b e o y

u x t h i s m n

w z a t i r a h

Word Bank

be   at
have   this

© Scholastic Inc.

Unscramble each sight word.

be at have this

ta

eb

hits

eb

isht

vahe

ta

eavh

© Scholastic Inc.

Word Bank

be
at
have
this

Use each sight word once to complete the story. Then read it aloud.

The monster was _____ the hat shop.

She put on _____ nice hat with dots.

The hat made her as happy as can _____.

"I must _____ it!" she said.

BYE!
GREAT JOB!

**Color the boxes with the four sight words
you learned in this set.**

be	and	on	at
the	this	have	is

© Scholastic Inc.

SIGHT WORDS
had, from, we, or

had

from

we

or

Hi!

Write the words above. Color in each box when you complete an activity.

1 Introduction	2 Read & Write	3 Read & Write	4 Color
5 Graph	6 Match & Find	7 Unscramble	8 Review

© Scholastic Inc.

Read the sentence.

The monster **had** a pal **from** Mars.

Write the sight words.

had

from

© Scholastic Inc.

Read the sentence.

The monster said, "Should <u>**we**</u> play with the car <u>**or**</u> the ball?"

Write the sight words.

we

or

© Scholastic Inc.

Use the code to color the sight words.

had — red
we — yellow

from — blue
or — green

Zzzzz

or	from	we	or
had	had	or	from
we	or	we	had
we	from	had	from

© Scholastic Inc.

Count and graph the sight words.

	had	from	we	or
4				
3				
2				
1				

© Scholastic Inc.

Draw lines to match the sight words.

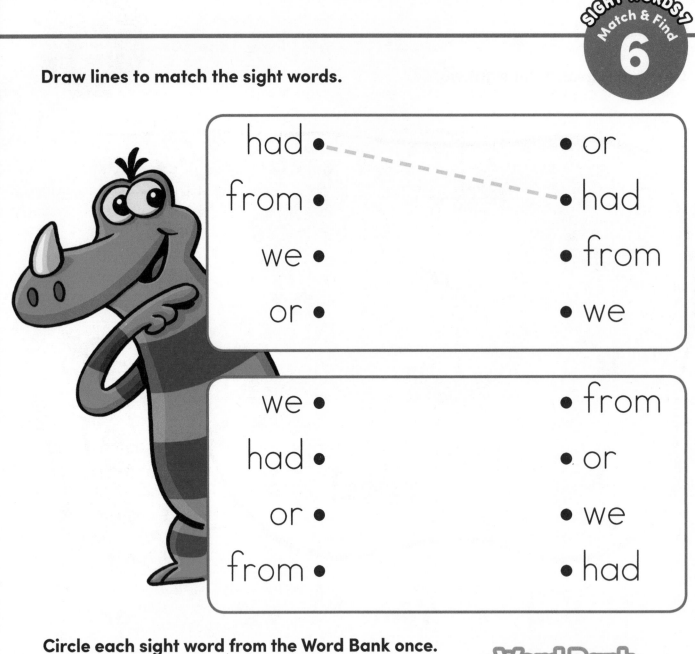

had •   • or

from •   • had

we •   • from

or •   • we

we •   • from

had •   • or

or •   • we

from •   • had

Circle each sight word from the Word Bank once.

k j v c o r y l

f g u x f r o m

m w e n a l i w

s u r i h a d o

Word Bank

had   from
we   or

© Scholastic Inc.

Unscramble each sight word.

had   from   we   or

mofr
_____

dah
_____

ew
_____

ro
_____

ew
_____

romf
_____

ahd
_____

ro
_____

Word Bank

had

from

we

or

Use each sight word once to complete the story. Then read it aloud.

The monster had a friend _____ Mars.

"I think _____ should fly to my planet,"
said the friend.

The friend _____ two spaceships.

"Want to go in the big one _____
the small one?" he asked.

BYE!
GREAT
JOB!

**Color the boxes with the four sight words
you learned in this set.**

is	we	or	of
from	a	in	had

© Scholastic Inc.

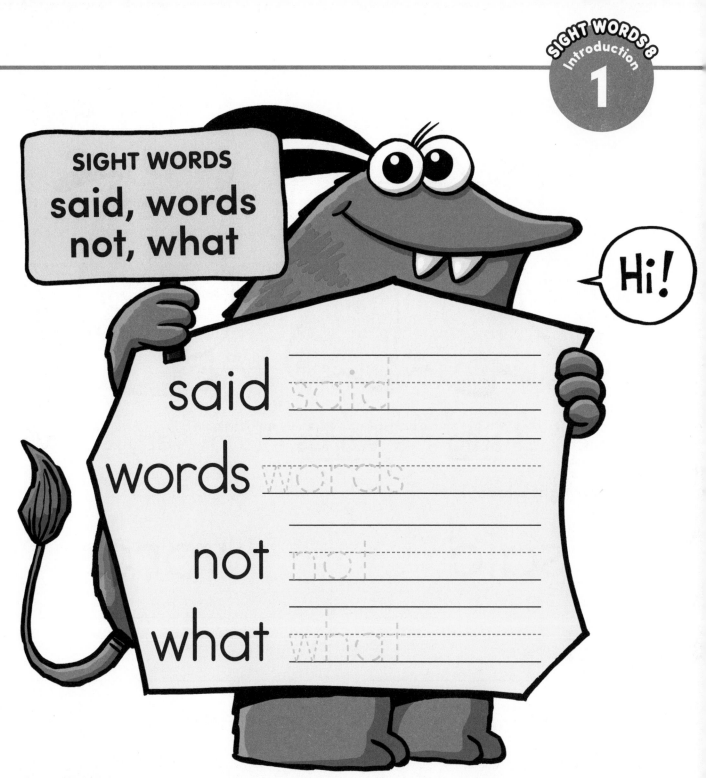

SIGHT WORDS
said, words
not, what

Hi!

said said

words words

not not

what what

Write the words above. Color in each box when you complete an activity.

1	2	3	4
Introduction	**Read & Write**	**Read & Write**	**Color**
5	6	7	8
Graph	**Match & Find**	**Unscramble**	**Review**

© Scholastic Inc.

Read the sentence.

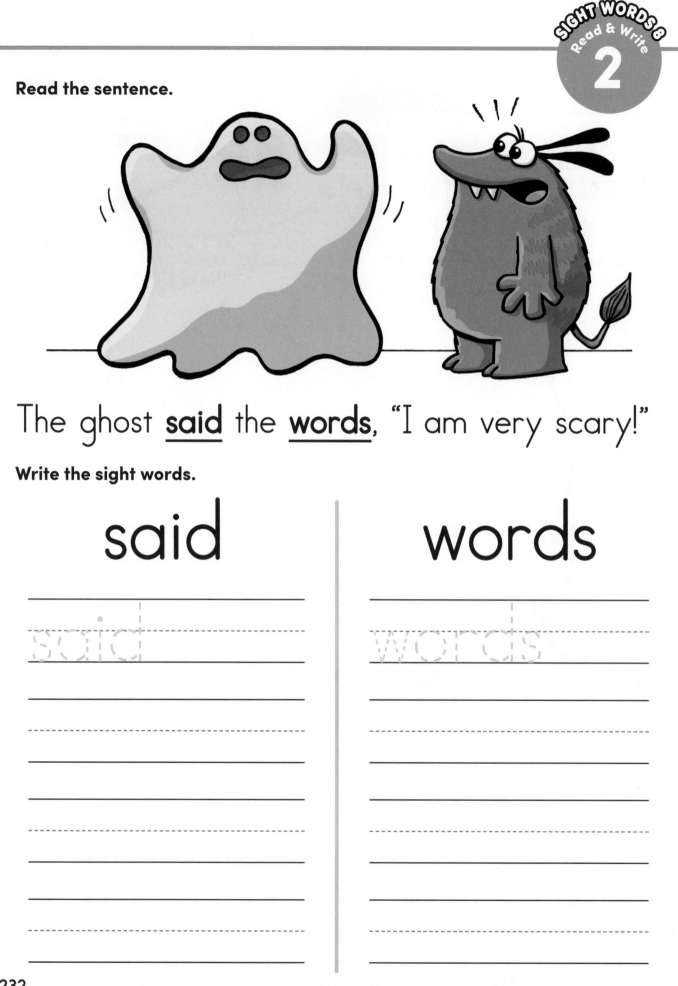

The ghost **said** the **words**, "I am very scary!"

Write the sight words.

said

words

© Scholastic Inc.

Read the sentence.

He said, "Guess **what**? I am **not** really a ghost!"

Write the sight words.

what

not

© Scholastic Inc.

Use the code to color the sight words.

said — red

not — yellow

words — blue

what — green

Zzzz

not	words	not	said
not	what	words	not
words	what	said	what
said	what	words	said

© Scholastic Inc.

Count and graph the sight words.

	said	words	not	what
4				
3				
2				
1				

© Scholastic Inc.

Draw lines to match the sight words.

said •   • what

words •   • words

not •   • said

what •   • not

words •   • not

what •   • what

not •   • said

said •   • words

Circle each sight word from the Word Bank once.

d s p w h a t n

t y z s a i d r

x l m n o t p a

a w o r d s e j

Word Bank

said   words
not   what

236

© Scholastic Inc.

Unscramble each sight word.

said words not what

sdorw

_____

awth

_____

ton

_____

dwors

_____

dias

_____

isad

_____

nto

_____

tahw

_____

© Scholastic Inc.

A Poem for My Pal

A ghost is scary.

A ghost says, "Boo!"

Are you a ghost?

No, you are
just you!

Word Bank

said

words

not

what

Use each sight word once to complete the story. Then read it aloud.

The monster wrote _____ on paper.

But he did _____ write a story.

So _____ did the monster write?

"I wrote a poem for my pal!" he _____.

**Color the boxes with the four sight words
you learned in this set.**

the	a	not	by
said	words	is	what

BYE! GREAT JOB!

© Scholastic Inc.

SIGHT WORDS
all, were, can, by

Hi!

all   all

were   were

can   can

by   by

Write the words above. Color in each box when you complete an activity.

1 Introduction	**2** Read & Write	**3** Read & Write	**4** Color
5 Graph	**6** Match & Find	**7** Unscramble	**8** Review

© Scholastic Inc.

Read the sentence.

Wow, **all** of the monsters **were** at the party!

Write the sight words.

all

were

© Scholastic Inc.

Read the sentence.

The monster **can** dance **by** the band.

Write the sight words.

can

by

© Scholastic Inc.

Use the code to color the sight words.

all — red
can — yellow
were — blue
by — green

Zzzz

by	can	by	can
were	all	can	all
can	by	were	by
were	all	all	were

© Scholastic Inc.

Count and graph the sight words.

	all	**were**	**can**	**by**
4				
3				
2				
1				

© Scholastic Inc.

Draw lines to match the sight words.

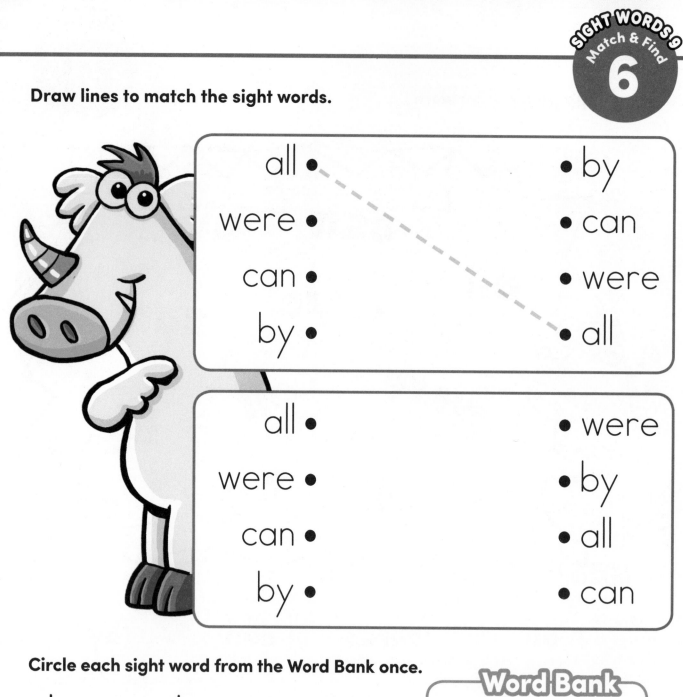

all •
were •
can •
by •

• by
• can
• were
• all

all •
were •
can •
by •

• were
• by
• all
• can

Circle each sight word from the Word Bank once.

l u z b y p o n
s d i w c a n c
p v a l l d s k
f r w e r e w o

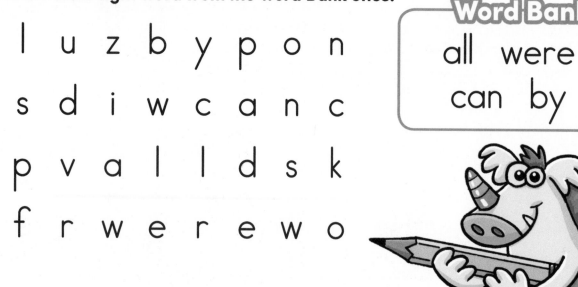

Word Bank

all   were
can   by

© Scholastic Inc.

Unscramble each sight word.

all   were   can   by

yb

_____

nac

_____

reew

_____

rewe

_____

anc

_____

lla

_____

lal

_____

yb

_____

© Scholastic Inc.

HAPPY BIRTHDAY!

Word Bank

all

were

can

by

Use each sight word once to complete the story. Then read it aloud.

The monsters _____ at the birthday party.

They stood _____ a very big cake.

The little monster blew out _____
of her candles.

"Now everyone _____ have cake!" she said.

**Color the boxes with the four sight words
you learned in this set.**

all	a	can	by
said	the	of	were

BYE!
GREAT
JOB!

© Scholastic Inc.

SIGHT WORDS
but, one, when, your

Hi!

but
one
when
your

Write the words above. Color in each box when you complete an activity.

1 Introduction	2 Read & Write	3 Read & Write	4 Color
5 Graph	6 Match & Find	7 Unscramble	8 Review

© Scholastic Inc.

247

Read the sentence.

There were two friends, **but** only **one** cookie.

Write the sight words.

but

one

© Scholastic Inc.

Read the sentence.

"I was happy **when** you decided to share **your** cookie with me," said the robot.

Write the sight words.

when

your

© Scholastic Inc.

Use the code to color the sight words.

but — red

when — yellow

one — blue

your — green

Zzzz

when	one	when	but
but	your	one	your
when	but	when	one
but	your	one	your

© Scholastic Inc.

Count and graph the sight words.

	but	one	when	your
4				
3				
2				
1				

© Scholastic Inc.

Draw lines to match the sight words.

but • — — • your
one • • but
when • • one
your • • when

one • • when
your • • your
but • • one
when • • but

Circle each sight word from the Word Bank once.

f g y o u r x o
s o n e r a c i
y p a f w h e n
h v a b u t o r

Word Bank

but   one
when   your

© Scholastic Inc.

Unscramble each sight word.

but one when your

tub

_____

hwen

_____

rouy

_____

noe

_____

eno

_____

btu

_____

nhew

_____

oryu

_____

© Scholastic Inc.

253

Word Bank

but

one

when

your

Use each sight word once to complete the story. Then read it aloud.

The monster got a ball _____ he went to the mall.

"I love _____ new ball!" said the robot.

I like it, _____ I want you to have it,"
said the monster.

"Thanks! You are _____ great pal!"
said the robot.

**Color the boxes with the four sight words
you learned in this set.**

but	we	when	of
you	one	in	your

BYE!
GREAT JOB!

© Scholastic Inc.

CONGRATULATIONS!

This certificate is awarded to

FOR OUTSTANDING ACHIEVEMENT

Signed

Date